Dream I Tell You

European Perspectives

European Perspectives

A Series in Social Thought and Cultural Criticism
Lawrence D. Kritzman, Editor

European Perspectives presents outstanding books by
leading European thinkers. With both classic and
contemporary works, the series aims to shape the
major intellectual controversies of our day and to
facilitate the tasks of historical understanding.

For a complete series list, see
http://www.columbia.edu/cu/cup/catalog/data/eps.htm

Dream I Tell You

By Hélène Cixous

Translated by Beverley Bie Brahic

Columbia University Press
New York

Columbia University Press
Publishers Since 1893
New York

Copyright © 2006 Éditions Galilée
Translation copyright © 2006 Beverley Bie Brahic
Originally published in France in 2003 by
Éditions Galilée, 9 rue Linné, 75005 Paris
First published in the United Kingdom by
Edinburgh University Press 2006

Library of Congress Cataloging-in-Publication Data
A complete CIP record is available from the Library of Congress

ISBN 0–231–13882–2 (cloth : alk. paper)

The publishers thank the French Ministry of Culture—National Book Centre—
for kindly granting a translation subvention.

Columbia University Press books are printed on permanent and durable acid-
free paper.
Printed in Malta.

c 10 9 8 7 6 5 4 3 2 1

for Fatima, without whom I wouldn't have
and with whom I have so lived and laughed
these twenty years
and who to conclude has deciphered the totally
illegible manuscripts
of these limbo things

Dream I Tell You

Forewarnings

They tell me their stories in their language, in the twilight, all alike or almost, half gentle half cruel, before any day, any hour. I don't wake, the dream wakes me with one hand, the dream hand tugs at the drawer to the left of my bed which serves as my box of dreams, noiselessly takes out the pad of paper and the felt-tipped pen pilot V signpen the one that writes so big there's no need to press, it writes all by itself, and one notes in the dark as fast as one can, in the margins, outside overboard, the tale fills the little boat to the brim. Docile I say not a word the dream dictates I obey eyes closed. I have learned this docility. The dream commands. I do. I have no thoughts no responses.

I have learned to block my attempts at escape. When I tell myself: this morning I won't write, not that, it's of no interest, I've got better things to do, jobs await me, forget it, tomorrow's another dream, right away the Dream says: you will do what you claim you don't want do this instant, write me, remember: never listen to your own voice. No arguing, no reason, follow the rule. You know your running away tricks. Do it before you think, before you read, before you are. You don't seriously think, says the Dream, that I have come to watch you take to your heels!

I have learned to give in and resign myself.

I note. The hand in the dark writes as best it can, hurtles along, getting off the track. Once it is done, the dream slips itself into the dreambox and I get up. Dozens of dreams later, maybe even hundreds, it comes time to read them.

My turn now! Dreams sleep deep. Now I contemplate their psychic faces at leisure, their long haunted bodies, and to be sure I discover their secrets.

These secrets, in this volume, I don't give them away. I never shall. They know too much. I respect their reserve, their twists and turns, I admire their disguises. They had to be well hidden to slip through the cracks in my walls when I wasn't in the least prepared to let them come. And then time passed. One day you can look the dead person's photo in the face. When one had just died my death, yours, jets of boiling tears kept me from seeing your faces. The months of tears are past. Now I can gaze at the photo of your face without flaring up, pitiless dream. I admire the tapestry of signifiers which give the mask its extravagant features. A whole night with Handel, and I never suspected that the stately accents are those of the haine d'elle, *the hate of her! I admire Freud's extraordinary power, first and last cartographer of these strange continents, the Shakespeare of the Night: he saw the movements and cosmonautic calculations of the whole genesis and anthropozoology of this world, its wiles and passions, subterfuges and stratagems, intrigues and plots, games of genre and species.*

Dreams are theatres which put on the appearance of a play in order to slip other unavowable plays between the lines of the avowal scenes: you reader-spectator are aware of this but you forget what you know so you can be charmed and taken in. You connive with your own trickery. You pull the wool over your eyes. The thinner than a razor blade that slips between you and yourself is an imperceptible vertical hyphen. You are a you [Tu es un tu].[1] *Do you see what I mean? Who is* you? *I am reminding you of the dream's delicate work; first it slips the invisible laser scalpel between the letters: t, u, t'es eu, tu,* [you've been had] *next between the signifieds Siamese twinned by homonymy: tu es tu* [you are you] *that's why, étant tu* [being you/having remained silent] *tu ne peux plus te taire* [you can no longer remain silent]. *As for the bistouri* [scalpel], *il bisse tout ris* [repeats, echoes, all laughter].

1. This section of the text plays on the multiple meanings of *tu* in French and on the sounds of the letters 't' and 'u'. Thus *tu* is both the second person singular pronoun, and the past participle of the verb *taire*, to fall silent; and *t'es eu* [t, u] means 'you've been had'. The second wordplay in this section is on the hidden meanings to be found in the syllables of *bistouri* [scalpel].

I'd better stop: I don't wish people to bristle at the thought of the philosophical and philosophicomical resources of the language.

I used to feel guilty at night. I live in, I always used to live in two countries, the diurnal one and the continuous discontinuous very tempestuous nocturnal one. But I didn't tell. I thought myself under false pretences in the one and in the other under false pretences differently, since I had but one visa for both. Furthermore I couldn't have said which was the main, the primordial one, having two lives and two temporalities, which one was the legitimate or the other. I went to the one that was perhaps the other with the surreptitious joy that gives the soul wings on its way to love, to lovingness, even without going anywhere save to the depths. I have a rendez-vous. What a delight to head off with high hopes to night's court, without any knowledge of what may happen! Where shall I be taken tonight? Into which country? Into which country of countries?

I used to fear losing my land of grace. Because Dreams don't come when they are called. They play God. One begs them, is all. Only their will is done. This fear came to me when, a beginning writer, I discovered with horror that this gesture, writing, which had become my life, permission, possibility, reason to exist was subject to the mercy and grace of dreams as an infant is at the mercy of the breast. What if they dried up? A few dry seasons came, I don't remember them, but

4

this happens, sometimes one's bed is empty, for it is a fragile soil, sensitive to the variations of the body, exposed to age-old circumstances. Dreams want a good mount. If the beast is harassed, they fly all the same, but with less force.

(Ah! What do I call 'force'? It is a matter of intensity, radiations, the physical emissions of the dreaming soul, of degrees of delight, almost always tragic. According to the state of the matrix, the dreams are naturally more or less apt to rise in the scale of the passions.)

If I stopped dreaming? I shuddered, I would crumble to dust.

But the gods do not forsake us, which is a mysterious thing. They are just like Him. They sulk, they hide? Right up to the day they come back. This alliance – what to call it – is incorruptible.

It makes for a kind of peace, to know they will be back. But this peace is war. For night in the land of restless and capricious populations is always war.

The world is terribly threatened, terribly anxious. Virtual catastrophes real plagues betrayals agonies deaths illnesses mutilations tombs hearts uprooted, children gone astray, the Bible and Aeschylus put together haven't more plagues and devastations. Is that me? That's me. But maybe it is you as well. It is certainly an extremely inventive hell.

Still, in these braziers, how I don't know, a strange pleasure springs from the suffering. Not the pleasure of the 'not true'. For it is all true during the dream. When I saw my mother die I saw it, I howl it, I eat the hot coals of anguish right to the death. But when the dream betrays me and realises my fear that you betray me fear so terrifying that awake I cannot feel its approach without promptly making my escape into illness or suicidal thoughts, when it keeps me alive in the midst of death itself, and makes me drink the dregs of passion right to the lees, this hemlock one cannot die from, where is the pleasure in that? In this and this alone: naked taste biting into the dregs. The joyless, atrocious, sad 'pleasure' is in the details of the suffering, in the suffering itself, in the taste you taste to the bottom where nothing forbids you to suffer, and each cruel dish, so relished, offers the heartbreaking pleasure of being able to feel.

For in the daylight country, one doesn't suffer the suffering, at least in our cultures, where raking the heart with claws and cries that rend your breast is prohibited, one is not allowed to draw the dreadful delight from the suffering, one is intimidated, one does not let oneself, one protects oneself, one deprives oneself, one cuts one's cords and one's body off from the mourning.

Only my paternal grandmother could grieve as in a dream on the tomb of her son my father. She is the only human being I have ever seen bellow to burst her entrails in broad daylight, like a cow giving birth to a calf already dead and cold and heavy, legs asprawl she gave birth to the tomb of her son. In front of my brother and me. It was divinely obscene. But she was a beast. Only in dreams does one give pain the food it demands, give it the freedom to pain.

To the calamities I allot their corresponding excesses: joys the diurnal world never gives. Those of love granted, exultations whose ecstasies only literature, daughter of Dream, allows us to feel at length. And the Return of the Dead. This way through night's magic corridors where our beloved come back to us alive, right here and with no blood tax at the border. Here death becomes what it is: only an almost interminable separation, interrupted by these rare, brief but ecstatic meetings. Without dreams death would be mortal – or immortal? But it opens a crack, is seen through, sealed up again. From its lands escape the ghosts who console us, mortals that we are.

This 'book of dreams without interpretation' began as a joke. It was at a dinner with Michel Delorme. Give me a book says this dream of an editor. For fun I say: 'What about fifty dreams?' And so it was accomplished to my amazement. It came about as a joke, nor could it have been otherwise. For however black and bloody these brief lives, dreams, may be, they are always also for the sake of laughter.

To the pleasure of suffering add the pleasure of the ridicule that surrounds the dreamer, in this case, the dreameress. Here's who I am too in reality? (For the dream unveils reality, does it not?) This woman on the verge of failure and presumption, now full of good will, now full of vanity? So be it. I accept this display of my foibles and weaknesses, my secret wounds, to which I owe my efforts at dignity and the sublime.

7

Fifty [cinquante]² *I said. Go and ask Freud why* cinquante. Saint? Sein [breast]? Seing [sign]? *I could have said sixty [soixante]:* soit [so be it]-xante, soi [self]-cente [a hundred], soie [silk]. *But I said* sein [breast]-qu'ente ... So be it. *After which I had to 'choose'.* Choisir *from* got. *Akin to Old High German.* Kiosan: *put to the test, taste. How to choose. There are two or three thousand of these dreams what am I saying! Two hundred a year on average, in ten years two thousand, in twenty years four thousand ... No, no. Choose? No!*

So one tries to come up with rules for not-choosing. Not counting the unconscious. But none of the rules work. Dreams of the year 2000? People would think there were dreams per year. Dreams used in books? Some of them are here. The rest was a matter of how they struck me. I dug in. Picked a card. Eliminated the dreams that I judged threatening or threatened with dangerously and inevitably erroneous readings or interpretations. I would be upset if a careless reading led someone to believe that I-really could have *really-had a* real *liaison with this or that monarch or great writer of this or that sex. Or that someone might believe* I *had truly killed or* wantedtokill *my son or my aunt.*

I have in no way 'corrected', censored, touched up the tales set down by my hand in the twilight hours. They are

2. This passage plays on various sounds and meanings that can be associated with or hidden in the syllables of the words *cinquante* [fifty] and *soixante* [sixty].

8

reproduced in their entirety, unpolished, innocent, such as they disported themselves in the preanalytic dawn. I could, for my own benefit, analyse them. Only I could do this, since only I have the keys. I do not do this here.

I could have collected recurring dreams so that in a series one could have identified the archetypes of my mythology. Thus there would be the dreams of X. or A. or J., hazel-eyed, male or female, bearers of the fatal sign; or the dreams of my son lost and found.

Analysis and literature I have kept at arm's length. These things are primitive tales. Larva. I could, by brooding on them, have transformed them into butterflies. They would no longer have been dreams.

I haven't evaluated them: I remain their dreamer. I am still in the dream that takes place inside me. No distance, however infinitesimal, allows me to re-read them as I can go over pages of writing, no third party has sat in judgement. For me they have been a source of care and troubles, but I do not know what they will be for you.

Collecting them I noticed archaic traces: as if my dream factory had been built in the 1940s, during the bombing, during the war; and this is no doubt the case. I remember dreams from my childhood, attempts to flee from the nazis into the forests. This continues. The nazis are still around. The nazis as nazis and as substitutes for other persecutors. Certain hints of violence which trouble the dreamer's relationship with her near and dear (hence asperities between Eve my mother and me) are also ancient history, I wish to say. There is no one with whom I have a gentler and more regular tie than my mother. Once we fought tooth and nail. These appearances of hostility are theatrical simulations (in which I still take other malicious pleasures). What do we know about the meaning of our passions, our heartthrobs, our moods, our faint spells and other symptoms? Hence I sometimes say: 'this business makes me sick.' 'It's your fault I've come down with pneumonia again.' But who am I to say? How many Vir, viri, viruses, virtues, real or fantasised are in league with tuberculosis/my father to lay me low?

Not everything is substitution and unrecognisable.

By the beating of my heart which does not lie, I recognise my mother the true or my love the innocent. Nevertheless, I must insist on putting up a sign here which reads: Watch out! Dreams!

These dreams almost always come with 'titles'. At the moment the Dream begins its dictation, it gives itself a name and announces it.

P.S. She who heroically deciphers these remains of battle, Fatima, sometimes turns up her nose in disgust. I rejoice. (Personally I feel only gusto.) The fact that she shudders means these bodies are not dead, or that these dead are still good and strong.

P.P.S. What about 'the order'? The classification, the sequence, the consequence? There is none. Readers will note *the dates and their indifference to chronological order. There is no disorder either. The dreams fell in place like the dead, pushing out of Hades.*

But there are so many of them, these denizens of the other world. When, imprudently and with neither clairvoyance nor blindness I tossed out the figure 50, it was also to be modest, some fifty of them, a trifle, a fistful from the side of the dune. Then ten thousand elbowed in, abolishing the illusion of choice. And all lined up together side by side in a single row. The date? Proves only the intemporality of the dream. All dreams are the same age, there is no hour, all are children of the Night. All I could do was let the first of the twins escape from the throats of the boxes filled up by the years. I said 'fifty', I say. But without my being able stop them a hundred popped out together, or rather a hundred or so. And how to cut, reject? I ought to have said: a pound, or a kilo. More or less. A big book or a little kilo of dreams. Consider the weight of each dream; or of a thought; or of a kiss; or of a squeeze of a left hand.

Immense dream   My father's daughter

Then when everything was arranged he came into the house. It was my father my young father, serious smiling, handsome. He glanced quickly around the premises, I had sent the cheques? Yes I say. I wrote a cheque for 10,000 for … I'd remembered it. The children? Everything is in order, despite all the work and the urgency I had seen to it. He was pleased with me. He sat down by the window I was incredibly happy. So we were to live together, at last, he was back the man of the house and of the life. Right away I started to imagine the rest. He had a lovely body, his chest bared a bit, full of grace. But he stopped me and told me, no, no don't make plans, I won't be staying long. I felt sad, I asked him questions. I feel I'll have to go soon. This return can't last. I haven't much time. I had to give in to his words. All the same he gave me and left me at least one very precious thing, and which was enlightening. Thanks to his attentive presence I had at last discovered that I was utterly my father's daughter. In everything we were as one, in harmony, there was a kind of music between us, everything I did he would have done, never in my life had I been so approved of, so recognised. It was truly as if we'd never been cut off. Even after he was gone I would be left with the force to feel that yes he would have agreed, he agrees.

First part of the dream

I was looking after the house which needed tidying, I saw to everything, the cupboards, on whose shelves I discovered artichoke leaves I'd forgotten to throw away, I cleaned all that while the children were out right up until they returned. There they are. Here's my third daughter. Now I have a last little girl. She'd just sprouted up. She even astonished me by coming in almost walking which is not so extraordinary since she's a year old, but was something new, and especially while talking a little which she'd never done before. She toddled in and told me – put me on your shoulders – in her baby voice. So my third daughter is small and blonde. I hoisted her up and sat her on my shoulders. Her long blonde hair tumbled over my face.

Come, we're going to go and have a look at ourselves I said – still playing I headed for the tall living room mirror. It was very funny. To see my face framed in that long blonde hair. The two of us made another very unexpected person. My daughter also was delighted by this vision. We made a single, long-haired girl.

How are we going to live now, I wondered, with my three children. It was all very well, I told myself, but if I wanted one of them to come, if I called Anne for instance and she counts on her sister to come, when there is one more child in fact one is less in control of one's family. I set to work, everything needed to be arranged, set in order for this new life. I sent the children out for a walk and spent the morning putting things in order.

28 October 1997

A long symposium

What to do I wondered to keep it from seeming like a prison, if you have to spend weeks in a place.

I imagined you have no respite save when you are able to sleep. But even sleep is no refuge for you awake in the same place, the same time, you have ceased to suffer for a few hours and the suffering of being in a time which stands still starts up instantly.

It was on the morning of the symposium that I was seized with anxiety. I had set aside an hour in which to revise my lecture. And the lecture was one I'd given before, the one I did with J.D. Nothing to fret about. We were with the family in one of those utterly sinister and poverty-stricken parts of the foreign city where the buildings are of coarse granite. Every now and then you heard a sharp crack in the East. The news arrived:

someone had just killed himself. You couldn't imagine a more sinister place. These are the apartments in which I began to re-read it. Eve kept bothering me, she was getting dressed inside out, under Omi's eye, talking. I went off by myself. I opened my notebook. Disagreeable surprise. My lecture was all but unreadable an erasure had occurred. Probably the last time I gave it this wasn't a problem it was still in me, still new, I remembered. I hadn't been put off by what showed up now on the paper: lines out of focus, minuscule. Peering closely at it I managed to make out a few of the erased words and I was able to write them again legibly but that took ten minutes. I leafed through. I noticed that I alluded constantly to one of J.D.'s texts: (a) what was the text, I hadn't made a note of it, probably I knew when I gave the lecture. It was too late to check. In any case I didn't have the books with me. Glancing ahead I saw J.D.'s lecture, which I'd written down, perfectly clear. It was mine I was missing. Oh, if only I'd done this the day before! If only I'd been my usual careful self. But no, I'd counted on having given it before. An anguish of shame welled up in me. Sitting at a little table I forced myself to decipher. A man came in and began to talk very loud. The local vet. Sir you disturb me. I have to give a lecture in an hour (I could have been speaking Chinese for all he cared). I insisted. Finally I told him to go out on the balcony and chat with my mother but since he didn't comply, I took my notebook, I left, I wound up and down the outside stairs, in search of some solitude. I saw a pair of young lovers sitting side by side. It was pretty. The girl was teasing the young man. The young man announced his name with pride.

Oh, how happy one can be, and me brought low by one puff of shame.

5 November 1997

I was surprised to see him turn up early, gay in the middle of the day, go into the bedroom, and head for the bed. I hadn't even tidied up since the previous day, I'd forgotten he came every day, there were the remains of our encounter that I hadn't put away, I had even forgotten to get myself ready. I had a little plaster on my toe. As it was so bright I went to draw the curtains, but he said I don't want to, I want to see you, your body is so beautiful stretched out in front of me, I want to see you while we make love, I was so astounded that I pressed up against him so he found me beautiful, already we were undressing, in a tender, wonderful bliss, everything was so urgent so loving so soft I was so surprised this dream was so amazing I woke up. Lying on top of me Thessie gazed at me.

27 December 1996

I disapprove of the mother with her strange way of caring for her little girl. In the street the child – no bigger than a cat – trots bravely along you should see her – I myself am forever on the run keeping my eye on her, but the mother a fortyish blonde isn't afraid. Back home, with everyone around the table, she's put out if little curlylocks gets too much attention. So she puts her to bed in one of the rusty brown cardboard drawers stacked against the wall. The little girl fusses from her drawer. I look on disapproving and anxious, I trust it lets some air in at least?

My mother is so sharp with Thessie it's no wonder Thessie is scared, she runs away, down to the basement. I scold my mother and remind her of the basics. Talk to her as if she understood and she will behave properly. I call in a soft voice, she follows me. I do have to promise her something nice to entice her out of that cave. I hold up a bottle with some white liquid inside, that's the best I can do. We go up the street now. I ask

her to follow me, my plan is to go to the Japanese restaurant over there, she complies, she follows me, I enter
the elegant premises with Thessie and we go to the
back where there's lots of space except for one gentleman already seated. The man is a little startled at the
company, but I ask Thessie to sit, and for now she is
behaving.

27 December 1996

At home at others'

Difficult weekend with Eve. We were at some people's house Eve and I, ill-received, Bice and M. Gendreau-Massaloux were there too. I tried several times to liven things up but it wasn't my house though I feel somewhat at home there and I wasn't in charge. Which is how I had the idea and the urge to go out. We could take a walk I proposed. But hardly had I approached the French windows when I saw it was raining. Worst of all was the night. To think I was in a room with a male guest sleeping in another bed. Next morning I was quick to leave, displeased. I met up with my friends again. I felt somewhat better seated at a table with M. G.-M. and Bice. I said I hated to sleep in a room with a man. That must sound like a proclamation of homosexuality I fumed. I would have enjoyed the give and take of intimacy and friendship. I went to the sideboard. I opened the door. The evening before I'd stashed a few glasses of iced white port in there that under the circumstances I had renounced passing around. Now I took them out. Still some ice, that was a stroke of luck. And I handed these glasses to my friends. Everyone needs a little treat sometimes. We drank. I longed for it to be time to go. My watch had stopped. This was a pleasant surprise. It might be later than it showed. It might be 5:00 already. We could start to think about leaving without seeming rude. What time is it, I enquired hopefully. M. G.-M. told me it was 5:00. Everyone pressed towards the doors. Shall we go? Everyone would be leaving. Such a relief. I told Eve we should take advantage of the confusion to slip out. But not at all she laughed at me. Don't forget I have to pick up Mme *** who lives in the vicinity, and it's still too early . We agreed that I'd pick her up at 6:30 and bring her back to my place. As a matter of fact I've a gift for her that I'd like to show you. It's a tablecloth I embroidered myself. Eve started to insist on showing off her handiwork. Pompously insistent, she embarrassed M. G.-M. who was keen to be off. As we watched she unfolded a piece of dark embroidery fashioned indeed with astonishing art. What she was capable of thirty years ago! I hadn't suspected her talent. Furthermore she was saying, it was magic, when one shook the little cloth spells fell out. Eve resembled a sort of modern witch, stubborn. When finally she folded her little cloth back up I returned to my wish to be gone from this dull and inhospitable place. M. G.-M., B. and I downed our little consolation glasses. What time is it? Let's hope we get away soon.

February 1998

An evening with Heidegger

My idea was to invite him to the University for lunch with just a few others. There'd be L. Labarthe perhaps and some young people, a tête-à-tête in fact, where you could really chat. Everything went smoothly. We sat at a small table draped in a white cloth. What I hadn't thought to check on, however, was the food, this I'd left to Eve and that was a mistake. Right from the start there wasn't enough of anything, and I began to be bothered by the smallness of the portions instead of devoting myself to the guest. I must say that very quickly, the news having got around, newcomers appeared, girls or women who sat themselves right down at the table in the places of the guests. Hardly had I turned my back when they were seated right beside H. I had to make two women get up quite sharply. I told them to take a seat behind. A second row formed. So much for the tête-à-tête. Next a lecture was being organised. Which wasn't part of the plan. Things were getting completely out of my hands. The whole University was abuzz. I was standing next to H., there was Sarah and somebody else, a hubbub all around us, people poured into an immense hall. We could hardly hear one another. H. leaned towards Sarah and said something to her. She raised her head. He kissed her on the mouth. With a sort of sly smile. She couldn't get over it. Blushing, vexed, humiliated. I too was stupefied by the incident. Had he found her attractive? In what way? Something about her lips? It was incredible and displeasing. S. might have reacted violently. Later I lost sight of her. Even I didn't know who was where – when I entered the lecture hall it was packed, people were squabbling over the seats in front and clustered on the podium in particular a woman in red just in front of the lectern. We wouldn't see or hear a thing. Her I got down at least. I thought I heard old Marguerite call me. Perhaps she'd saved me a seat in front. But I couldn't spot her. Finally I took a seat in the sixth row. Someone behind, a woman, forbade me to sit there, having kept it for V. I informed her I was Hélène Cixous and I had organised this event, but she didn't want to hear. I stayed put. I wondered if the public had understood what H. was talking about. He told me that everybody had caught his allusions to their own local affairs. When I make peace, he told me, it is implicit in the concept of peace that it be universal and perpetual. Really? I said. He was very sure of himself, very upright in his dark suit, always that touch of irony a little cold and sure of himself.

1 December 1997

I wished to be alone with X to talk about my work and I went off into the tiny room with its armchairs. To my annoyance I saw a strange woman ensconced in the armchair, with just the person I wished to confide in. I protested, I informed her that I found her intrusion most indiscreet and uncalled for. She said she was a fan of my work – not someone who knew nothing about it. Besides she told me I was discussing *Déluge*. She stood up. She said she had been working on the manuscript. I expressed astonishment. She came back lugging a notebook that seemed to have been hacked to pieces. I look. And yes astonished I recognise – yes my handwriting. But where can it have come from? I have a brother who loves me, she says, so much that he is willing to rummage through dustbins. What?! Yes, it came from the apartment trash. I could not therefore claim to be the victim of theft or pirating. I had thrown this notebook away. It was not mine any more. Impressed by the young woman I suddenly realised that I was not safe from indiscretions.

My correspondence with G. crossed my mind. But of course I don't throw his things out, I reassured myself.

I'm going to have to be careful about my remains in future. At the same time I was touched by the passion of my fraudulent reader.

30 December 1997

A night without Thess, but not with without you. I've only myself to blame if I'm without you. First of all at the time you were supposed to come I was not quite ready, I had reached the stage of debating what to wear, when I hear your ring at the second door, the door just for you. I leap, where are you my love, who is knocking at the door, I race down vast corridors, terrified I might miss you. When I finally get there, but when, but where, I have managed to pick up en route a totally undesired presence, A. is with me, and I haven't a notion how to get rid of her, I can't picture it. So there we are the three of us. You wish to rest, the time is short, I owe you this repose and I desire it, I lead us finally into a bedroom, and here's how we arrange our-selves: you lie down and I curl up behind you like a spoon I am tight against you and A. is behind, next to me. I squeeze you, as if that were one of the normal ties of friendship, now we form a single flesh, as if that were the simplest thing in the world, little by little my mind goes blank, I am no longer attached to anything but you, in an ecstasy no one can break, not the people who come in nor the presence of A. nor the manner in which she might interpret such close friendship.

5 January 1997

The symposium was taking place in this old inn building. There was a reception in the course of which I filed past Chirac who stood in a corner like a leek, and to whom I didn't say a word. He was part of the wallpaper. I filed past very straight elegant impassive.

The accident happened. How I don't recall. My right hand found itself cut off. Naturally I thought about a graft. It was teatime. We were chatting all of us sitting at little tables. I had put my hand down on the table beside my plate. It's a very pretty hand, fine-boned elegant with delicate nails. What surprised me was that no one seemed to notice that my arm did not at that moment end in a hand, maybe because set flat on the table the stump looked like a kind of miniature closed hand, but still. As time passed, I was anxious all of a sudden. Maybe by the end it would no longer be possible to have my hand sewn back on, maybe the hand which is alive and beautiful would be dead. I bent over my hand. A crumb of dirt under the nail of the baby finger, I tried to remove it. That's when I started to worry about it. I rose, I took my hand, not even the children seemed frightened.

I took a few steps with Yvette S. who gave me a small bouquet. She told me about her two months in prison. It's true I'd forgotten she'd had to undergo the shock of that. Because of my hand, I listened to her. We went out slowly, she drew the double doors shut behind us carefully. Don't close them, I say, my cat is inside! She won't be able to open them. With my left hand I took hold of the little wooden latch which broke unfortunately and came off in my hand. It will be difficult to prise it open with just one hand. The door grew transparent and I glimpsed Thessie who was searching for a way out through the door of another room.

13 January 1997
Osnabrück

I looked at my watch and yelped. Four o'clock! The time I was supposed to go to the theatre! And here I was, in this immense property with everyone going about their business. And I should have been home, and I should also oh horror have taken the call from Irma. Irma! I must ring her immediately! And then, quick, the car! I barked orders at everyone, at Anne, at the others, quick, come on, quick, we're leaving, and Thessie! Find Thessie someone! Frantically I searched for a telephone, and my address book. No number for Irma obviously. There was still old Marguerite. I grabbed the antiquated phone. Dial the number I shouted to Anne, I dictated it to her, all the while scanning gardens and halls to see if I couldn't spot Thessie. Finally I get Marguerite. Call Irma I shout. Let her know. Marguerite answers there is always music on her answering machine, then she's getting on my nerves, putting things off. I hung up. Better if I run to the house – if ever – I ordered everyone to get ready to go and I ran to hunt for Thessie. On a little embankment a rusty creature with bright fur curled up sleeping catches my eye – a squirrel! So pretty! It was snoring. I was spellbound. Three or four others lay around it curled up heads down or on the side. And standing off to the side of this ravishing group, a big duck with a long neck. No doubt animals try to gather to sleep. I went off again in search of Thess. I called Thessie Thessie! Someone gestured off into the distance, she is there, she is over there, the man was pointing at a mainly white cat. It's not her I say. Yes it is, it's her. Wary of my short-sightedness I went all the same. The creature was as it turned out three colours with some black and also and perhaps rust I say once I'm in front of her, I took her in my arms, she was long-haired, this wasn't Thessie, she was big nice not so pretty, I could have but I was looking for my Thess. I called and called. It was late, I was going to miss and make others miss the theatre. I called Anne was calling me, she thought Thessie was probably next to the car.

17 December 1997

I didn't believe it. We were really off to Crete together. This was in two days. I hadn't really packed my suitcase, since I didn't believe it, but still there it was lying open in front of the house, the small bag for short trips. You on the other hand were ready. We were out in the street, you believed it. You had already put on your travelling suit. The all-white suit which spoke of summer, you were the fabulous travelling character. Basically I couldn't get over the fact that this was about to happen. We were leaving, two days before departure you had already left your home and there you were, big as life. I was the one who was unprepared. I pulled on my bathrobe, I crossed the street, I went to put a few things into my little suitcase. I debated I began to think what I should take. Light things. My grey jacket. I should dump out all these things I'd packed by mistake I thought and be done with it. I decided to cross back to you. You are on the other side of the street, in the car. I make some futile gestures – a few steps, I come back, I put on the bathrobe-coat again. At this point you flapped a newspaper in rage or irritation. You showed it to me. That's it, it was in the papers! There was an article – but fawning – with a big headline. He's leaving, he's going here – there, they described your trips like a rock star, it was gossip column stuff, not nasty. I saw nothing much wrong with it but you had nevertheless been found out (but not a word about me). While we were talking I think of my suitcase I'd left open in front of the house. I look up, I glance around. It's not there any more. But a few metres off a normal-looking, fairly tall, hefty man walks calmly, my suitcase in hand. At the top of my lungs I shout: Stop, thief! stop thief, and I began to chase after him, and you too stop thief my suitcase that's my suitcase, he has stolen my suitcase. The man breaks into a run. The man wasn't letting go of the suitcase. What was I going to do? I was in front of him. I shouted to you (you were coming along in your beautiful white suit): shoot him! and I added so that you would understand: Take out your gun and shoot! shoot! The man grew scared and dropped the suitcase. And everything calmed down. I began to talk to him. Why had this well-dressed man stolen? Now that everything had been returned to me I didn't hold it against him.

And you, you'd been ready to pretend to shoot.

18 November 1996

The real child
(the trustful child unaware that one sometimes forgets about her)

Happiness is having a little girl: what a delight, a lovely little girl alive and kicking. Already capable of doing all the things a baby does. Bouncing in bed. She's awfully active. My beautiful little girl. And bouncy. She wants to play. I catch her just about to tumble off the bed in her excitement. My beautiful round bare-naked little girl. She's all I can think of, bustling out so gaily to run an errand, all I can think of is my baby, as I run to the bakery with Eve at my side, I left the window open, the house has an upstairs. That way from below I can hear her, my little girl, prattling. She's all I can think of. How old is she? Almost a year. Ten months maybe. When did I have her? I don't remember. I must have had her last year. Probably I didn't know right away that she was a real baby. A real baby. But now she has taken. She is just like a real baby. A lovely little body, strong. Now the baker concierge is telling me he needs a key. So he does. Should he have to go up. But I haven't time to do that now. Rushing out was risky: I figured my girl wouldn't fall out of bed if I was quick. But no lingering. Over my shoulder I fling: Eve'll give you her key. Impossible to make copies. Out I rush. Through the window I hear my real baby really crying. Oh my joy, my anxiety. I call up 'I'm coming my baby,' to let her hear her mother's voice. 'I'm coming.' And now how to get back up? I stand at the foot of the little house with its upstairs in which the so-unexpected unhoped-for extraordinary baby is alive and crying. A real child. Did I pop to the shop next door to see if Eve was there, or is it only the dream popping its head into the so-crowded shop?

I've already summoned the elevator, without waiting for Eve, I am filled with anxiety, what if my baby were about to fall, but I can hear her crying through the window, she is still there, still alive.

14 May 1990
Beethoven, Rêves de la Bien-Aimée

The innocent

Why my god how did I manage not to look after the darling child all day long? What could I have been thinking of? Only at the end of the day do I come to my senses and remembering, shudder.

And go in search of what's needed to make a bottle. No one lends a hand. The place is a mess. In vain I ask Eve for help. A saucepan. To warm the bottle, but it's chaos. Full of sobs fully awake now I pick my way around the obstacles, frantically thinking of the child left alone downstairs, who must be desperate. She won't have seen a soul or had a bite to eat since the first bottle this morning. Obviously, the child's unaware she's been forgotten. Poor innocent. I imagine her alone, in the silent empty room, left in a time without limit, unaware she has been forgotten, I imagine the baby innocently suffering (believing this is normal), unprotesting. The worst in fact is that the baby hasn't cried, hasn't called. Not a peep all day. It haunts me. Up above, however, the struggle against material obstacles continues. While, terrified, I search for saucepan, bottle, milk, I talk to my brother, we recall the story of the mongoloid child (who wasn't mongoloid).

If you want a real bottle, you won't find it I tell myself. Time passes violently now. Instead of hurrying, putting an end to the child's solitude at least, and especially reassuring yourself that she didn't suffer too much, a whole day after all without a thing to eat. What's urgent is to go. At which point I took a cold bottle, it would have to do, and hurried to the bedroom. There was the child in her cradle. When I opened the door, she smiled at me, the innocent. In the shadows, her little face had shrivelled, aged, what love I felt for her, the weakened, trustful child who cannot know that a mistake of mine has caused her to suffer for so long. At last the second, if makeshift, meal, which she should have had hours ago, has come. She was smiling at me, from her cradle. Like the feeble memory of a child. Ready to let herself be loved, fed. Her wizened, trustful look twisted my heart.

Dream of the marvellous photos

I was absorbed in the photos. There were some very strange photos among them. My eye was first drawn by a photo taken in the street, as if in front of the Oran Officers' Club, a photo so astonishing that as I looked, the people in the photo ran still, a blonde girl before coming to a halt at her place in the corner of the photo. There was one picture I didn't like: me in profile on the balcony in Oran avenue René Coty probably. Who could have taken it and when? Probably A. just before we left the avenue? And I was standing (black and white) sharp face between the shutters, cheek a little emaciated, the nose aquiline. I peered closer, yes I had on my small old glasses. I was baffled, why hadn't I removed them? But, underneath, was the response. This was another street photo, in Oran, taken during the war. You could see a few soldiers – five or six, with their round helmets, outfits not very soldierly, this photo too was extraordinary, it had been so well taken that the men still ran, in the street, trying to overtake one another, along the metal railing of the Officers' Club, his body rocking a little, there suddenly, I saw my father. And it was *me*. Exactly. That face with its high forehead, cheek a little hollow, tiny eyeglass, looking young and serious. Ah, I understood why A. had snapped that strange photo on the Av. René Coty. Look! Look I say (at table, heedless of the company) the photos! You see the people moving still!

16 August 1992
Beethoven

It's a nightmare city, the one where Eve and Anne live at the moment, an ancient, thickly-populated city.

I wanted to take the elevator, the worm-eaten metal elevator. Anne reminded me that she was scared. What if it broke down etc? Fine, take the stairs. The staircase! It's wood, hundreds of steps you can't walk on, rolled up tight, backwards. The man ahead of us curses, and warns. You have to climb, slide, crawl, what's more the staircase sprawls over everything, no way to go up it. Besides, this staircase is a cemetery. In here's where many of the former inhabitants are buried, in the dark wooden steps. As we clamber and scale, we are shown remains, papers from tombs. These are big sheets of paper with rebus-like drawings. A gentleman hands me a sheet, which I decipher haltingly. Doctor Green – followed by a fairly good-sized drawing – then I make out 'has – three worms' (there are three worms). Ah! yes. So that's what that dreadful staircase was like.

10 March 1992
Beethoven

The battle took place in the courtyard, in the big square, between M. and X. I don't know why we'd left Simon there, in the corner of the square. I kept an eye on him. He didn't budge. Probably he was asleep. I doze off. The two boys rolled over on one another. Of course I was still a little scared they might bang the baby there in the corner, the very small too small baby. (There'd been a discussion about it a moment earlier, with whom? In which I had already been pained to see it lying there, a sponge and no bigger, how old? It looked about a month old, but I counted up, it was born in May, that makes five months I say.) The battle dragged on. I dozed off. When I came to the battle was over. I had slept half an hour. It was a mess on the plateau there. Everything had changed. And the child? I couldn't see it. Full of anxiety, I began to search for it. It wasn't in the corner any more, I went over, I searched, I couldn't rid myself of the thought that it had been struck perhaps and pulverised, they must have struck it a blow, I found only a sponge, a body? And that, those

wilted little flower heads, were they?? No, no, I found
nothing, nothing you'd recognise, no identifiable
remains. I searched in vain. I asked the boys, they'd seen
nothing. I was still anxious. For sure, but without
saying, it was dead, it'd been killed. Then I went over to
the little house which had been fixed up for me. It was
a delight, a corner house, already decorated with
flowers. They had run real wisteria along the trellis for
me. I touched the yellow leaves, was it artificial? No!
Flowers everywhere, along windows and walls. A
dream place on the new property. Then, as I visited this
place, with a heavy heart I saw the rest, behind the
house the duck pond, and a view of countryside, but
to the side of the path, poop, whose? I tried to believe
it was donkeys, but it was humans. You can't have everything. There were the ducks. I went up to the pond.
They were swimming vigorously – six or eight
perhaps. And now one of the male guests arrives with
a plank, tries to kill one, bashes it. I was furious. I
shouted. Stop! The fellow had no intention of stopping. Who was I? The daughter of the house. I told him:
touch a duck and I'll have you thrown out on the spot.
(I didn't know whether I had the power, but I would
try.) The man yielded. I turned on my heels. I met my
mother. This business still weighed on my mind. I asked
if she'd seen Simon. She who'd been across the square
during the battle. No she says. I spoke of my concern.

45

Promptly she accused me. It was my fault, etc. What! I say did I put him there? Besides he was very much alive. While I slept then? Hadn't she kept watch? We fought bitterly. But above all. But above all the thought wouldn't go way I chased it away, it came back, he was dead, we'd lost him. I had no proof, I didn't want to believe it but I was in the grip of a dull ache. Over and over I told myself: it's just six months after all, Time will pass. We'll ('d) just have to make another one. I tried to forget, I tried to accept, but it was impossible, it was a nightmare you don't wake from, I could neither think of it nor not think of it. And I said nothing, the horror was tucked away in the bottom of my heart.

10 November 1990

Such a desire to go to Oran

The mere idea that the train might pass within sight of the city made me wild with joy. I was told the city had horribly changed, but the person who'd been there also said that the city was yellow and orange and that she didn't care for such garish colours, which I love. So I took the train overjoyed at the thought of seeing for the first time, far off, even for a minute, the colours of the city of my birth. To get there in the station we had to take catwalks over the platform, and in the middle of the catwalk, come back down the staircase. We arrived on the platform, lugging suitcases. We took the train. I was in the compartment with Y., that former doctoral candidate, a tall fellow, fairly handsome, with a stony face. The lady said how for food they'd given her bread (showing with a gesture) the size of a marble. Oran no longer lived as it used to. But I thought only of its beauty.

On the station platform, the lady went to look for a wicker hamper. This was what passed for left luggage. I saw several hampers stacked in a corner of the platform. Granted, they got locked up, but it would I felt be easy to take one. Nevertheless it occurred to me that if someone stole my luggage I wouldn't have lost anything essential. The main thing was Oran, that I so desired. In the train I found out there'd be an hour and a half lay-over between going and coming back: it would be a round trip. So I would have an hour to plunge into the city of my birth? A wave of feeling swept over me. I saw myself penetrating to the heart of the city, near the Place d'Armes, I saw myself in the midst of coloured matter, in the thick of neighbourhoods.

9 March 1992

With the dead, in the underworld

the one where the dead live and all the reprobates, especially homosexuals what was I doing there? I had descended. Now I lingered, I watched, but was also part of the noisy, restless crowd. In the land of the dead, everything is just like up above, except for the sky. It's underground, down below, but the world is just the same, you have the sea, a vast dark blue sea, in which people swim. And there are cafés everywhere, people meeting, an end-of-the-world atmosphere, people search for one another desire one another, there is a sort of gaiety, here is a merry-go-round, a meeting in the round where, among the crowd, I recognise Maurice, and someone else from the Soleil. These people are going to act and work, I believe with Peter Brook, they call me, but I won't go, I tell myself that even if they aren't too unfamiliar, some of them are going to recognise each other. J. has come, it's the end of his visit, it's time for him to go, I'm a little flustered by the crowd. J. goes off. He goes down the hall. To the right there's a very narrow corridor. It's over there. He ducks down it. He seems to be waiting for an elevator. And off he goes saved! Why oh why didn't I go back up with him!! What held me back? Kept me from going up with him. From thinking of it? I could have jumped in after him. And returned to the outside world! I dash off in the direction he took. There, on the left, a button in the wall. Yes, this is where it is, here's where you push if you want to take the elevator that goes back up. So now I know.

I come back to the land of the dead. In a hallway, I come across a sort of shelf, two babies abandoned there. Not moving. Each has a number on its back. One is number 40, the other? X and I discuss the meaning of the number. Is it a date of birth and abandon? So one has lain there for ten years? No they say it's the age of the parents rather – which makes them rather old. Or maybe it's the number of a generation. One comes with photos. A photo showing a German-looking interior, all in wood, with Christmas trees, a family. I can hardly keep myself from making off with them. Done. I take them. The two of them, the one bigger and sturdier than the other, the one a few months old, the other tiny. They are not good-looking. They are lethargic. I get busy finding bottles. Here is a big bottle, brimful. I pick them up. I put them in two baskets. I wrap them up completely, like bread in a napkin, I cover their faces as well, I hide them, and I go to hunt for some bottles. It takes a while, they're not easy to find in this world. Here I am exploring. Finally I find some. When I get back what an awful shock! My shelf's covered with all kinds of clothing people have thrown there, not seeing what was in the baskets. Ah! no doubt they've suffocated?! I yank everything off, I throw it all over the ground no way I'm going to waste precious time putting it away, who cares what people think. And I rush to the baskets. I open! Oh – they are dead. Faces inert. Lids closed. But no! They come back to life. I hold them, I lift them out, they are alive. No they waited for me. They are happy. They smile. And see, I have the bottle. I pick up the biggest one. Does he want it! How hungry he is. He drinks. I bought tons at the pharmacy just in case. He drinks he drinks, he's alive he's alive. I take the bottle away, his body arcs, he wants more, drink drink, oh what joy this return this hunger. He's saved. Now I must change him. It's been ten years since he was changed. I hold him against my shoulder. A woman arrives, looks everywhere, stricken, my child, rummages around, sees I have two. Doesn't dare think one of them might be hers. Grows desperate. After all she left it, I think. But finally I relent, I can't, if there's

51

a mother, let myself take this child without remorse. I lie. Then I resign myself. Suddenly, to her astonishment, I say: is this yours? (She who believed it was mine that I was looking after, that I loved.) Here. And I give her back the child I loved, which was already mine and which loved me. Now only the tiny one remains. Everything is for him now. I pick him up. At this moment a wretched little woman arrives, forlorn, who appears to be searching. Not the other mother? But this woman doesn't believe in it, she is too wretched and apathetic, she searches without conviction, sure she won't find, off she goes, I haven't budged. I keep the baby. Quick now, live. Where to find something to eat. Just then my friend goes by. I follow her. I would like to find a pharmacy, buy some milk. My friend goes into an incredibly luxurious – and expensive – hairdresser's. I make out an immense salon. I go after her. To my astonishment she takes a seat, she is going to have her hair dyed. I can't get over it, her? Yes indeed. People fuss over her. Me standing there with my tiny baby. You don't know I asked, where I could find some milk? Meanwhile there are big sinks here, warm water. I am going to be able to wash this child no one has washed for ten years. Making myself at home, I go to the nearest sink, and fill it with lukewarm water. The baby is frightened, stiffens. I almost have to use force to bend it, then I put it in the warm water, where I wash its little body, I run my hand everywhere. Then I lift it out, quick a towel. At least he is clean my little darling, at least a little regenerated. Now I just have to find milk. It's a start. I'll manage.

5 September
Beethoven

Tour of the Concentration Camp

where I have arrived in the course of my trip to the
United States. Visit to the gas chambers at Auschwitz.
A splendid visit, you enter, the crowd, in a hall.

To begin with, seen from outside, it is a reconstitu-
tion, a sort of small white-and-varnished-wood oblong
mausoleum. On the front, a few white oven knobs.
That's how it worked. This knob switched off the
lights. Darkness killed as much as the gas. Omi and I
looked at that, then I went in. The entry hall was a surprise. I'd never have expected this glazed, lavish-
looking, spacious (I'd imagined narrownesses) sort
of vestibule with faux patios, steps. Right away I
attempted escape. Instead of climbing with the crowd,
I veered right and hid in a niche of cement, a hollow.
The crowd climbed today's yesterday's, doubly mourning, yesterday's anguish revived, I gazed at the ceiling

from which the night would come. People camped all over the steps and everyone joined in a sad funereal picnic, unwrapping slices of bread and butter, all already weeping and wept. I was in the vestibule of the awful mystery. And all the while I was thinking, so this is how it is, this dark temple, the people climbed, mothers nursing babies, one ate, one worried, higher up probably it led to narrow places, but here, basically it already looked a lot like a funeral parlour.

We're getting ready for a breakfast. There are the butchers who take their holidays in March. As for me, I'm going to look for Omi. Omi is so old, so old that now she's become tiny. But she is up, dressed, elegant. True, it's a job for her to stay standing, for she is so small, so light, so old. I kneel down I take her in my arms. All she's got left are reddish hairs, on her round head. I love her deeply, tenderly. I sit her down in the dining room. Since she's small, when she walks by the table, her head is at the level of the tabletop. Later when she's no longer around, we'll say: she came up to here, and this will be difficult to believe and to imagine, such a tiny but complete person. But that's how she is. Once she is seated, I notice that in moving around, a few strands of her hair shifted place and are sticking up. She'd hate her hair to be untidy. Discreetly I leave, to look for a brush. I go next door. There's a brush there with big rubber bristles, for baby. I take this brush, I slip behind Omi's chair, and I smooth the sparse, unruly locks.

The little dog is crafty as a child with me. I know how to bring it up so the world marvels at it. In the hallway, when films are being projected on screens perched high up in the niches, I take the little dog, and I lift it up. On two legs like a baby, it watches as if it understood. It plays with people too, slides between their legs, etc. Oh – while I'm busy with the dog I catch sight of two yellow birds making love in flight. Rapidly, without hesitation, I slip my arm under their two little bodies, and I show the dumbfounded audience the two yellow birds billing and cooing on my left arm, as if it were a branch. Naturally, this doesn't last, for our love-birds soon fly off.

22 September

In spite of his death, my father

I had put my aunts up in the lovely big house. Night was coming. I heard some noise. I hurried towards Claire or Deborah's room. She had thrown the French doors wide for the night. I told her not to do that, because it made a dangerous draught, in the house. She'd have lots of fresh air, the house was so big, and besides with the door open a thief might come in. I had to explain our way of doing things in the house.

I busied myself looking over the premises. I was restraining my emotion. My father himself was in one of the rooms, my father, despite his death. I knew he was staying there. I want to speak with papa, I tell my cousin, feeling the emotion well up inside me. To want to speak to him was extremely audacious. But later I will and I'll hear his voice. For the moment I felt him nearby, in the left part of the house, a marvellous guest, as if in the left side of my chest.

High in the mountains

First of all I see a sign carved in stone at the park entry: you are entering a Hebrew establishment, a foundation. That's what I learn. We go out, here we are on the slopes, which our hosts scale at top speed. I force myself to keep up with them as they rush up hill and down dale, along steep, bushy cliffs, for fear I lose sight of them. The one who's thrilled is (Pif Pierre) my little brother, who's managed to encounter a wild goose. There he goes down the mountain straddling the big goose with its blue-grey feathers, delighted, and yelling I want a refrigerator and a wild goose, because the goose is a fairy, the goose, he's already got it seeing he's on it, he gallops down the mountain, bellowing his wishes, and you know, there's every chance he'll get them.

Does one change men after such a long time? I've lived with my brother so many years I never give it a thought any more. Even my mother thinks this normal, it isn't that nothing could change, but well the grand-mother has come to consider it normal, there are the children etc. But for Anne on the other hand things are different. She can still change. Last night, for instance, that's what happened. It was a tragic night in any case, in the heart as we were of nazi country. The world violent, cruel. In the tunnel black as a mine shaft I saw nothing but the feet, or not even, of wretched, whipped humanity, and all one saw all down this chain were wretched furtive gestures: under my eyes, a foot scratching at the earth, scratching and scratching. Would there be something edible maybe? But nothing. Only black earth. Ah, somebody's found something: a stealthy, robber hand, darts out and filches a crust of bread lying off to one side, someone else's bread, which flicks out of sight. In the black night Anne and I were in the room. And in it, fleeing, her suitor had appeared, the one she doesn't love. She didn't make a move. He was left outside, exposed. I believe he had lain down on a cot. Suddenly, a *horrible* cry. Horrible. In the night. A cry of anguish and incredible pain. The axe! The axe! I get up, I run towards the cry. I see the man stretched out in the dark with an axe planted in his chest and who cries, who cries who cries! The axe! I'm going to die! It's true. They've planted an axe in him! The nazis probably. What to do? Anne can't decide. I rush out. To remove it I have to cross the room in which my aunt and Fernand sleep like logs. I put a little light on, too bad. I cross their room, I run to the door I go to the front of the house, on the black grass, still the cries 'I'm going to die', the despairing cries. I make it. I'm going to save him? But how, he's drenched in blood. Not a hope. I try. This pitch black. The agony. Anne comes later. Now, the axe is out. People around. The man is sitting up on his cot. He's surely going to die. He has blood on his mouth. I see his silhouette in the night a young face. In profile one might say a little coarse but endearing, a shock of cropped blond hair. And he smiles. Dead? No. But surely going to die. These are his last instants. Anne could? Love him? No. Besides come too late. She makes excuses. There was thought of removing the dying man to the bed, with a hot water bottle. Him, more at ease, sure to live now they've pulled the axe out, smiling in the night with blood clots in the corner of his mouth. After all, is it so sure he's going to die? Who knows? In any case, he's happy. Yes, at this moment, alive, people around him, he believes again. The whole area's infested with nazis. Walk to the end of the sandy avenue that leads to the sea, in the hope of finding food, and two loom up with guns. One has just time to drop behind a clump of bushes which don't in fact hide anything. Simply one isn't standing. Danger lurks everywhere.

1 December 1991

Wake in a house turned upside down during the night – that's what's happened to me. I get up and to begin with when I want to go to the bathroom, I have to squeeze past piles of cardboard boxes, there's something big in front of the window. Only later when I start to move the heaps of paper do I see what it is: the big radiator from my bedroom shoved over there. But also, why is it so dark? I grope into the gloom. The curtains are drawn. That's when I feel real anguish. Has someone broken in during the night? Who can come into my house and turn everything topsy-turvy? The incredible exhumation under my eyes: dusty sheets of paper, I recognise my work on Joyce from forty years ago, sheets of notes, things that have never since come to the light. But all of a sudden, turning around, I catch sight of the silhouette of Eve asleep on the couch in the front room. That explains something: she must have wanted to get up, not sleep in her room and therefore shut everything tight in here where everything's always open, so as not to be bothered by the light. I feel somewhat reassured, so there wasn't any prowler. I go along the narrow hallway, this house is also the old one Avenue René Coty and when I wish to go out into the entryway I have difficulty pushing the door as if it had rusted and swollen with time. This is worrying. But that's not all: when I finally manage to give it a shove, I see the white paint has big earth-coloured blotches on it. As a matter of fact so does the wall. I tell myself that B. is going to have to get busy cleaning this up. Furthermore right in front of me in the entryway lies an enormous mattress. What on earth is that? Someone rings. I open to Sarah. I'm going to have coffee with you I say. Sarah unrecognisable. Hair reddish-coloured sprinkled with glitter she looks ten years younger she's a knockout. What a success. Right up to the moment she pulls a strange face and from the side it's not pretty at all. I really would like to go to the kitchen. But I have to get past the cartons the boxes. B. arrives. Time to clean up. I tell her to help me put the drawers back right side up in the chest. What surfaces gives me the creeps. Old clothes, a complete shambles. Armoires full of old things. Oh look! beige leather ankle boots from ages ago. Into the bin! B. as expected is so little help that I don't get the drawers back in. Awake, Eve turns up too she starts to rummage which makes a mess, I show her the drawn yellow curtains to explain why it's so dark. She is baffled. Now

Eve digs up slides of disinfectant ovules she tells me we have to throw this out before anyone sees it. It's been ages since I've made use of such doses, it was forty years ago. Monsieur Donon the guardian arrives. I am still not dressed and I haven't had my coffee. I'm beginning to feel the effects of this. Behind Monsieur Donon I discover two guys, one of whom, enormous, is pulling his clothes back on. He apologises telling me his photos didn't come out, he has to come back and do them again. I no longer know who he is, but no doubt someone I must have received. I note his features up there with the feminine hair and especially I see tiny breasts under his thin T-shirt. Is this a man woman?? When he's ready he waves and goes off with his friend. Taking the monstrous mattress. That at least didn't come from here. The place looks brighter already. Did you see that guy? says Monsieur Donon. He had breasts I say. Falsies says he. But I could tell they were real. I'm beginning to feel sad. I tell B. to make coffee. For all the good it does. This is a day that is going to go by without me being able to start off on the right foot. So much to be done, tidy clean fix.

This is what happens when one begins
shifting the past around.

28 July 1996
Or

Papa

I was in a corner of the big waiting room. Back there, invisible papa was seeing patients, he took x-ray after x-ray. I was working in my corner, without moving, so as not to disturb the past. That's why I asked the helper if he would mind fetching me some letterhead from my study which is the room on the left over there. Men were coming out. I saw someone I recognised slightly, who was coming out looking half relieved half cast down. I gave him a friendly tap on the shoulder. How are things? He made a face. He told me things weren't so great. I told him we too had had a coloscopy, because when my father'd had his cancer, he'd wanted to protect my brother and me. We started talking about childhood. My father worked and worked. Right up to the moment he finally emerged from his examining room on the right at the back, in a lab coat. I called him, I spoke to him quietly but firmly. Can't you stop for a while? At least over lunch. No, no, he couldn't, so much remained to be done, I spoke to him nicely, these things had been done so long ago can't you I say stop for an hour? You have to live a little. I insisted. I told him: it's that I've come too late, and I haven't been able to teach you how to stop for a while. Had I known you earlier (I thought of my mother but) I say like a lover full of self-confidence, I would surely have persuaded you to listen to me. He was listening to me and smiling. A gentle, kind, serious smile. Stop this once I say. Come, let's go for a walk together, take me with you the way you did once remember, when I was little, you took me along to, it was the one and only walk on which I had been alone with him, I saw it over there in the distance, in the mist, like a story, like a myth, you took me along to, I wanted to say the name but the name was gone, standing in front of my white-coated father I sought it with all my strength, way off in the depths of the past in the damp sea mist I was with him, for once we were alone together, I couldn't find it I tried and tried, this name this name, it's the key, I must say it to catch the tiny speck of time rolled up over there in a precious shred of mist, for if I can't name it I will be unable to prove that we did it once and could do it again. My revenant father waited in a gleam of docility. Like when we went to – suddenly the name came back to me like a knife tearing through the mist, brutal, real, true, having occurred. I shouted: to Cap Falcon. I had it!! I have it. In a stroke the two scenes joined – the one of old when I was so small and which had only happened once, and this one. To Cap Falcon! And I burst into tears, I wept for everything I wept for the life which had gone unlived, and my father who couldn't stop for lunch. Now, will you come? Now that you are dead, are you going to go on doing x-rays all day long, as if you were afraid to die and leave the task undone?

Saturday 15 May 1996
Or

I have a brand-new baby. It's been delivered to me. I decided to go home on foot, which may be foolish, for the way is long, and above all the baby may not be wrapped up enough. Its body is completely swaddled in linens, but its tiny head is bare. But I am sure I can protect it from the elements with my hands. As for food I offer my left breast. For it is a baby animal and finds the small teat the size of a cat's which is under the nipple, at the end of the gland all by itself. That's where it sucks. I myself had no idea I had this little teat there beneath my breast.

These days I live in the big neighbourhood school building. As Fatima, who is there too, says, the place has its charm. But the first night I spend there worries me: the neighbourhood boys make a terrible racket out in the street. Without their shouts one suspects the neighbourhood would be perfectly quiet. Here I am again in the vicinity of a boys' school I fret where I was hoping for calm. I put visitors off for example that old couple of Algerian Jews who are interested because yesterday I wrote a play quoting lots of words in Hebrew or Yiddish.

All in all I tell myself they are interesting words, and once they've gone, I try to make note of them. I go out in search of Fatima, to whom I express my concerns. But she tries to make the best of the place I am just getting to know. It's true that there are little trees in the halls. I even wonder if I mightn't have a small room to myself for my work. I take a tour around, it is early, no one's there yet. Fatima asks if I wish to check over the publisher's cat-alogue. We need to decide if we want to reprint the books that are out of print. We go into a classroom. My beloved sits down at the desk. Fatima puts the catalogue on the table and shows me the list. In a way I'm pleased to find myself quite by chance close to my love. This is one of the secret scenes of our life that I adore, these times when we act as if we didn't know one another and we stay very close without speaking and without looking at one another, like strangers. But this time the pleasure is partly spoiled for me by the negligence of my attire, feet bare, not a speck of make-up wearing a house dress. Fatima says shall we republish *La Jeune Née*. No I say. Then suddenly I change my mind. Yes. Above all I want not to be under the eyes of my beloved, for not expect-ing to find him here, it's a disagreeable surprise, and I make a quick exit. The empty halls are bare but there is a little something about this place.

22 July 1996
Or

The white horror of having been condemned to live over this clinic. Am I ill? Why did they chase me out of my home and assign me to residence here? The staff is nice, to be sure, when I climb the blank staircase back to my place, and I meet the blonde and yellow nurse who smiles, but I'm wondering what I'm doing here. Up top the rather chic restaurant keeps itself busy, run by the lady of the house a pretty woman with a slightly metallic voice, who keeps the place open at all hours despite her husband's death. My table is at the back. I keep an eye on the owner's two little boys, hyperactive twins. And behind me I find a few items of children's clothing. Skirts and such. This is where my domain begins. Are these your daughter's clothes? I enquire. Yes. May I put them away? You know how small and make-shift it is in my place, a former apartment, cramped and twisted, and not even cleaned out. Horrible to live in not-my-own-place. The lady shows me where to stow the clothing: in a buffet with big cardboard drawers, all askew, already full what's more. Now I explore this place to which I have been condemned. This is when I discover it has some modest but vital, and unlooked-for advantages: outside corridors, that run along the building's sides, but out in the open, very narrow, but airy. Right away therefore I can imagine a garden, a row of pots, that is, a few tulips and on one side there's even room for a narrow flowerbed under a glass overhang. I cajole and plead with the manager, if he could and then there are bits of wall here and there, I could hang two or three pots if he would be so good as to find me some nails.

So little by little I climb towards life, in the strait-jacket of my prison. I don't waste an ounce of air or sun. I explore I bring to light.

27 April 1996
Or

The camp – it's the theatre, thronged, people rushing in all directions. I'm going to leave. Outside the threats have Arab Indian faces. That's when a sand storm blows up suddenly. For an instant one might think it a gust of wind. But no it's the wind of the apocalypse. A non-stop attack, against which one is helpless for this wind blinds us, blows its grit into faces with its intolerable thick hard breath. First I put my hands over my glasses, then I try to pull my fur coat up over my face, this would protect me if I were able to lift it, but the wind is like a moving wall which slams into us, hard, impla-cable, I lift the coat like a tent I try to slip behind its skin shield, the whole camp is gripped by the storm.

14 May 1996
Or

Whenever I have a day with my love I rise in the morning with the day inside me. He lives nearby. Out I go all dressed to meet him, in the café on the wide avenue. Oh! To see him drive up in front of the café in his lovely black car, is it a Mercedes, how proud and how in love I am he pulls up for a moment in front of the establishment and climbs out. I show him to Omi, see how elegant and how handsome he is. Scathing and mean Omi took a jab at his shoes: what dreadful shoes she says, thick and ugly, he's always got the wrong shoes she carps. It's simply not true I protest, they are very lovely very dear little boots my love is elegant and well-dressed. The battle continues. Omi denigrates him right up till my love innocent and smiling stands before me. Suggests coffee before we go off. Proudly I offer to park the beautiful car. I like to be at the wheel of *his* car and to drive it properly. I gather up my many layers of clothes. I'm always getting tangled up in them coat shirt jacket inside outside, now I'm ensconced in the wide seat, but a little encumbered, I invite my brother to climb in on the passenger's side and I take off. Then oh then, I drove a little ways, and now I can't stop!! I lean on the brake, nothing, did I lean on the brake? Where is the brake? Where is the brake?? I get scared. I beg my brother to help, through the layers of fabric I find nothing. It comes to me that I ought to fling myself out onto a sidewalk to stop the car. It comes to me that damaging my love's car is a double misfortune no I can't stop, I fear an accident, the car is moving I leave time day love in my wake, at last at the bottom it seems to slow down, I make a U-turn and decide the answer is to go back up and return it intact, and so late so late, but how to accelerate? The car climbs like a tortoise, I can't find the accelerator, in vain I push I push, nothing happens, will I get through the green light, slowly we climb we go through, I'd been gone for hours when at last I get back to the café. Mercifully my love is still there at the bar astonished smiling and kindly. I confess my misadventure, my shame. In vain I beseech my brother, he has collapsed beside me and is no help.

There I am all tangled up in my clothes having seriously spoiled the start of our lovely day! Ah, but we still have lovely hours ahead of us. My love's plan is to go somewhere. Will we go to a hotel? Will we make love? O mysterious sweet elusive day which is there and escapes me and promises everything on condition!! Let's hope let's hope.

27 October 1995
Osnabrück

A brief moment of grace

Were we on a boat? We were passing through a foreign country.

Suddenly up above, where the family was, my father. He was staying for a while. We had gathered round the children and were having a family conversation. We were discussing bodies. I looked at the little ones. With my mother. The little fellow, with his puny body, but still he had plump little buttocks. My father said his little buttocks were like apples. A good way to put it. Everyone looks up to my father. He's the expert. This is the truth. He turned towards my mother. She too had had such pretty little buttocks. I listened to all that changing time and place in the family. My father was there, up above with us in the close family circle. Tall, slim, handsome, and masterful, always. And in his gaze my mother was the young woman she'd been. And me?

Would he have a word for me? Discreetly I drew apart. My father was saying – I could hear him – Hélène didn't have those round buttocks, no – she had a pyramidal body, the Egyptian body, flat buttocks broad shoulders, in those days it wasn't fashionable, I drew further off I went down the stairs, my father was speaking, he was saying I had the shape of a statue, that classical form, which in those days people didn't appreciate, and which later they did, and while his voice sketched me, I moved straight harmonious tall under his words with my beautiful, different shape. Once downstairs I paused. Someone was going along the corridor. My father is here, I say, he has come back. Already the thought of the end of the return entered into me, the great joy ripped apart, he had come for a mouthful of time, two weeks, he was going away again, I felt the need to say something to this any-old person, she didn't listen, and he was going away, I was left with my anguish, telling myself the news: soon he is leaving again. He had just had time to sketch me, to dub with his glance my rare and elegant form. A sob would shatter my breast.

6 November 1997
Osnabrück

Rue de la Libération

I decided to go straight to Libération to find out about the results. It was a Sunday. Once upon a time in my far-off childhood I had lived in this Clos. And I went towards it and I remembered. It was I believe to the left on the outskirts of the village. I hurried on, on foot initially, not a soul in sight, in a broad street where to my distress and amazement great groups of shops rose up one after another amidst huge restaurants behind facades of multi-coloured frosted glass. All the stores sold shirts and clothes but they were empty. I supposed the shops had tried to attract customers with the combination. Every thirty metres up popped another one but whatever the location, a street corner, there was no one but the owner there looking out. Fleeing this sinister avenue I turned left. I had on elegant new shoes, not having realised I was off on such a trek. Flat-heeled. I hoped I would make it. Maybe Libération was soon. The neighbourhood in which I found myself was deserted, it had that faded stuck-in-time dusty red brick colour of old neighbourhoods. I walked west a long ways – I was growing anxious because my feet were baking. Never mind I'll get there, I hope. At last I saw three boys playing on a street corner. Thank heavens, for I no longer knew which way to go as a matter of fact I'd reached a fork in the road. Maybe both streets led to Libération, but I couldn't be sure. I no longer remembered. Besides, nothing was familiar to me now. I stood facing this corner. I asked the children if they knew the street. Yes they told me you take this street (the right I'd been about to go left) then they told me to go two blocks straight on, then right and down at the end was Rue de la Libération. Having named the streets they asked me if I'd find my way. A bigger boy kindly offered to go with me. These three boys were the only living things in this embalmed neighbourhood. On we went, past one street then two then to the right. And there to my surprise lay a field or a wood but bare that I'd never have recognised had I really lived here once? We went our way, because of the season there was nothing. My companion extremely kind and courteous, we went straight on endlessly. He told me that at Libération they only received visitors once a week on Monday afternoon.

Damn! I wasn't going to stay around another day! I had left on the spur of the moment without thinking to call, make sure, make an appointment. On I walked I could no longer turn back. I hoped they'd still see me. The landscape was unbelievably gloomy and empty. Out we came at last. The traffic artery in which we found ourselves felt less desolate, because built up, but just as empty. My brother and I came to a halt in a sort of café. My brother looked at the books I had with me. They were about my father and his magic of old. Seated opposite me, my brother said he wasn't wild about the title *Or*, that it wasn't right. I promptly agreed, adding that in any case I had no intention of publishing these worthless books, so he shouldn't worry. At one time I might have considered it because they meant cash 5,000 or 10,000 francs it is not insignificant when one is in need, but I'd given up on that idea. So we spoke alone in this deserted place.

5 October 1997
Osnabrück

The tomb of J.D.

The day had been painful for St. hadn't stopped pestering me, the ghost of my son St. kept prowling around until at last I told J. that my whole life I had been plagued by this ghost, that I'd had to live with this haunting for decades, without ever mentioning it. It's that it's the south, and it's here in Nice in '88 that the poisoned dart first struck me. At the end of the day I found myself in a rather grassy green garden, a large square carpet and that was the cemetery. In this garden plot with stones that didn't show down in the right-hand corner of the scene stood a sort of tall piece of furniture with cubbyholes of dark wood. I ran my eyes over it – the cubbyholes had names on them. I realized that they corresponded to presences in the garden. As I gazed, suddenly my eye fell on the last little cubby down at the bottom on the right where I saw two white letters one above the other. At the bottom D. Above J. and beside J. in white letters the word Tomb. In a flash I understood! This indicated J.D.'s tomb. I had glimpsed the secret, I was sure of it. Thus, he had planned his tomb in this southern cemetery, here was the answer to the question so often tossed out, he had already decided, settled, this is where it would be. I bent down, I saw two little buttons next to the letters. I pushed, a spring clicked and behind the letters *tomb* a small cavity appeared. Within this minuscule box a speck of brick earth. That was it. The tombstone would be clay, baked earth – this was a fragment – perhaps the tomb already existed. I snatched the fragment. I broke off a fingernail-sized crumb that I wrapped in my handkerchief. Theft accomplished, I slipped the rest back into the little box and sealed it up again. I had found the last resting place. I looked innocent, I buried the fragment of J.D.'s secret tomb in my pocket. What I hadn't been given, I had taken.

16 February 1999
Le jour où je n'étais pas là

Bombarded

Eve had just left. Omi, Anne and I were preparing to go. I held Omi's coat for her. Suddenly the lights went out. A sad yellow ray trickled through the windows of the little dining room. Boom! a thunderbolt crackled over the city, unbelievably spread out, on and on. Heaven's lorries, I thought. The sound rolled, rumbled, swelled in the air. Then, out of the sound flew a plane. It was a plane this sound had as if preceded by several years. The plane a speck in a conflagration of boiling light, a sheet of yellow fire unfurled through the streets, right to the top of the world. Bombarded I say. A bombardment I say. The word scudded off my lips. The City's public address system spoke. The voice went up and down the streets saying – I reconstruct – chopped – drowned out – swallowed up – this is a drill. It is a rehearsal for the war – trying to be reassuring. The simulacrum drowned out everything. We couldn't hear ourselves speak. We were swept away in the roar of the plane. It had happened. The thing.

Le jour où je n' étais pas là

A long and complicated stay in an establishment in Portugal, that is in eastern Tunisia. To my surprise the weather's chilly. The hotel is almost a city. I recall a few episodes. Having retired to an apartment I await the return of the others, gone for the day: this is Y.S., a woman with whom I have struck up one of those quick friendships; someone comes along, it's Eve. I have no desire whatsoever to go back out to eat. My homebody side. I would like to dine in my room. Nevertheless, Eve and I go out. Traverse gigantic corridors thronged with people. A distinguished-looking Gentleman turns around and says something I don't catch. – What? – How's the dictionary coming? – Oh! yes, a spectator. I said in public that a Tibetan dictionary was needed. With a smile I say it's coming along. Sometimes we have to clamber over chest-high, draped barriers. I get over the first one easily enough. At the second foolishly I try to slip underneath and get myself all tangled up in the fabric. When I finally emerge I see clusters of Arab children behind. In front of the corridor windows are baskets of luscious cherries. The children call out, begging for them. I scoop them up and quickly, surreptitiously, hand them out. Only afterwards do I think that these glossy red cherries must have come from a hotel resident's basket. At the end of this very long crossing, a flat-bottomed boat. Eve and I head for it. At the wheel, the pilot is an old man. He casts off. Where are we going? He navigates through dirty water, between hulls. He wants us to see the sunset. Eve and I exchange a few words. The man stops, thinking we want to go back. No, no, I say. *Bueno, bueno.* I don't know if that's what you say in Portuguese, but the old Arab understands, he starts up again. Finally we come to a halt in shallow water. Children wade. Eve disembarks. Here the water ends in the mud of a sort of channel. Turning around, I see Eve jack-knifed under the yellow water. I cry, I leap out, she is fine, I set her up again. She says she wanted to pick things off the bottom. But don't you see this water is totally polluted and full of trash, you'll get sick furthermore she is soaked, filthy hair glued to her scalp. What folly! It's in the Jonas family (the folly).

18 February 1998
Le jour où je n'etais pas là

87

A delivery

I was in the crowd waiting in front of the restaurant.
The owner came out and announced the names. But
there was grave mishap. I saw several little women in
brightly coloured, big round haiks, as if for an Arab
wedding. But no gaiety. The woman who was the
owner appeared and called for the Doctor. Everyone
looked at me. I didn't budge. She insisted. A doctor,
urgently. I'm not one. Finally, yielding to the pressure
of her error I went inside. Brusquely they told me: she's
going to die. Who? A young woman who was miscar-
rying or giving birth. I am not a doctor, I say. And I
went inside. Stretched out in the room the mother in
yellow-orange – blue – veils, did indeed lie wailing,
dying. Face agape like an immense grey mouth – she
was grey. I went up to her. I saw moist puffy hands.
I trusted myself. I took those burning hands in mine.

I squeezed hard. At least I could comfort her. I bent down and said: here I am, we'll go with the contraction. The contact of my cool hands and my words calmed the woman. From then on I was part of the birthing. We embarked on a wave, it went on and on, I guided and supported, the woman emerged safe. A pause. I felt death going off. I spoke with the young woman. I said we'd do it. Meanwhile the restaurant people were looking at my file. They exclaimed. I said I wasn't a doctor. But for the woman's sake I added that my father was a doctor and my mother a midwife. And that I had done deliveries. So we kept on and each time I felt life winning out. I asked if she was completely dilated. But we were coming out of the horror ...

21 September 1997
Le jour où je n'étais pas là

Small invasion

We were in the little sitting room and Omi let in the following caravan: a small cart, a woman, an old woman, a bunch of children, on the cart bundles and bags and a big dog not to mention the rest of it. It's the dog that ticked me off: a big Alsatian. I bounded over. Out! The cat's here! Omi had opened, as I can well understand, from an old instinct: a Moorish woman turns up, it's for the midwife. But that's ancient history. In fact these people had knocked at the gate in hopes of being taken in. They explained they'd been given a day (eight hours?) to be gone. They were trying their luck in the neighbourhood. Who had kicked them out? Their man as a matter of fact. Later I vaguely reconstituted their story. But for now, and pronto: the dog out – tough. Tough if he leaves. I showed him to the gate. En route there was another dog, unless it was the same, gnawing on some big bones in the garden. I grabbed the chops not without disgust for they went along with the head of a black dog or sheep and I showed the dog out. The black sheep too. Beat it! Let them stay at the gate or not but no way to keep them in here. I saw children rollicking in the street. I went back in. All these people would need to be properly trained. As a minimum, fed, that we could do for a few days, it would make a fair crowd at meals. It's not the money, it's the work above all, the writing, the peace and quiet, Thessie, that were endangered.

What would I do with this gang, at least three rowdy boys, a baby'd been set on the hedge. Things looked difficult. And all because Omi had opened the gate by mistake without even asking. Had I been at the door, I'd have asked what they wanted, I wouldn't have just opened.

9 January 1998
Le jour où je n'étais pas là

When a sin comes back (its memory) you absolutely must bury it. How to bury the memory of a sin that comes from a distant past? I shut it up in a clay pot. Then I dug right into the cold hard ground, deep down. Without of course telling anyone what I had in the pot, then I stuck this pot the size of a little quart saucepan into the ground and I covered the hole in the ground with ice for a long time, and that despite the presence of people who had no inkling what I was ridding myself of in this little improvised coffin.

Le jour où je n'étais pas là

Tragic vision. The fugitives and their guide or protector a handsome sporty young man arrive on the top of the cliff. Did he dive? Did he fall? It seems to me he had a rope in the beginning. Or could he have wanted to look for something in the bottom of the water? The dreamer below on the brink of the abyss. Suddenly the catastrophe. The hero is about to drown. He struggles, as if trapped underwater, all you see are eddies and bubbles at the crater's surface, you hear him shouting under the water, weep almost. And the ones above, they do nothing? Nobody leaps into the black water to save him? He is still alive, a ring of bubbles, no one, he shouts feebly from the depths of the dark water. The dreamer who has no power over the scene bends to the black water, and piteously, lamentably, dips her hand into the thick water, perfectly aware that if by a miracle in which she doesn't believe the man could grab her hand she can't imagine how she would pull him out. But plunging her arm in the water, she comprehends the horror of the scene. The water is black and thick as molasses, full of black leaves and dense shadowy vegetation that must hopelessly have entangled the one who had the misfortune to venture in, blind water murderous power. But with their strength, their ropes, the people up above should have tried. Did they give up right away, put off by the difficulty of the task? Yet when the first rings of white bubbles appeared on the surface of the dim funnel, they could still have found him.

Slow drowning agony death in black duration, atrocious groan of farewell

Whereas the 'death' of Gregor cannot be compared to any (none at all) death she suffered no agony, didn't have time. Where it was no one knows, it was all New York and anywhere. The announcement of the 'disappearance' was Kusch's letter. Wake up. The play is over. It is done. The way one wakes from a dream in which one shouted, suffered, pleaded, moving from the abyss to bed in a single movement, like turning a page, and leaving all the suffering in the world on the one before.

'Just a dream', the terror of this expression when it designates a fragment of reality. A shard of reality. You have to feel the thickness of the water.

The suffering remains. The passions, the embers are not extinguished but they are without hearth, the desire, the anguish, the fear, the anger were addressed to someone. But the man has vanished; he has not left, is not dead, nor is he not on this earth any longer, he has never been there.

Pain, Dread, Love, Fear remain. They won't ever go away. They entered my life in the Beinecke Library – settled down in my memory, taking New York for setting and for character a fictional being as powerful and as powerfully fictional, of a substance as unreal as Gregor Samsa. Once the play is over, and the lights come back up all of a sudden one understands that the real characters, the immortals, are those faceless powers, Love Fear Death Suffering.

10 August 2001
Manhattan

Naïveté

To my horror, with a childish sort of naïveté, J. clambered up over the sill of the narrow window, and out he went, walking on air. He's going to fall, he's going to kill himself I saw, and caring not a whit what people might think about my feelings I howled like a madwoman, I thought my throat would rip, to attract attention and give vent to my dreadful despair. He meanwhile had just noticed that he could neither walk on air nor go down it like a staircase. I read his astonishment and I shouted and shouted, not a second to lose. Then halfway down, someone by the name of Clement heard me thank God, saw J. free-fall, intercepted him with a push and sent him back up a ways. Now it's up to me I have to catch him, wild with anxiety I leaned over the ledge, please please let me catch him, I grabbed him by the shoulders and with a colossal effort yes I was able to drag him safe and sound back onto the ledge – later exhausted I lay beside him. Fancy thinking he could walk on air – like a little boy.

17 August 1998

The bad cat and the madman

How distressing to know a dangerous madman is after us. All the neighbours are on the lookout. Someone is determined to break into one of the rooms of the building. We all try to watch out. I am very frightened for I sense his presence as I go through the rooms. Each time I open a bathroom and go into a bedroom I shudder. I return trembling to my own lodgings. All of a sudden there he is. He looms up in front of the barred window. A very tall man with a ruff of beard dressed from head to toe in a pink tunic. I summon my ghosts my father, my love help me! A struggle ensues at the window. The man is under control. I bring him an electric razor. He shaves, docile. I tame him, I train him. He's really a madman, a wretched savage. I treat him gently but firmly. I can't let him stay in the house. He can and must stay in his own room is what I teach him. You must go home. I order him to go, I show him the door. This is not an exclusion, it's the law, you must learn to stay in your own place and not intrude. I nudge him towards the landing. It's a mad cat. On the landing. Now I show him his way. How will he cross? Will he manage to find his own room two floors down? But this cat is looking more and more like Thessie. Its intelligence astounds me. I open. And she crosses the hall, finds her door easily, slips in. There – all's well that ends not too badly.

26 July 1998

A trap of a festival

I have already lived through this frightful situation: the head of our State gone mad, turned criminal and we must kill him or be killed. On the last day, the two of us play cat and mouse. I pretend to be docile and powerless. I know however that the battle for life or death is at hand. The plan is for a great trap of a festival to which all the kingdom's important people have been invited. Did I sleep? Maybe, but with one eye open. At dawn the telephone wakes me – the head no doubt, I want to get up but I must fight off a kind of torpor, a drowsiness as if I had to break a spell. The telephone stops ringing, he must be on the line still. I pick up the phone. I hear – not the head – but the polite shy voice of one of the teachers. Monsieur Bergougnoux here he says, in a soft voice. You know I am ready, you can count on me. Ah, true, part of the population is aware a coup d'état may take place. And what do I do? I say nothing, I say thank you, I say we'll get together in a little while whereas I should have told him to come join me immediately. But I am hazy with fear, witless. The head with his grinning devil mask shows me around his house, the décor, the arrangement of the food, all of which seems fine and good, but I saw the two serpents dozing on the ground, the great big one and the little tiny one, their steel grey bodies slim and viscous, death waits there, then he takes me to view the outbuildings or the grounds. Sheets of water everywhere through which I walk gingerly for at every step one is in danger of sinking. Huge staircases of water cascade slow motion, black as escalators.

Nonetheless, when the guests come, I'm on the alert. Either the head will spark a massacre and the world will end, or seeing the counter-attack is ready, he'll shrink into his shell and that will be that. P.F. arrives, my son, he's a great little ally. He follows me. What I fear most is the snakes. While I chat with the head of state in the great hall, I eye them. The head is in between, of course. Suddenly I grab a not very big stick and slam it down with all my might on the little snake. Without killing it, unfortunately. The beast ties itself in knots loops, divides itself up, slithers off, I even go so far as to try and trample it to no avail. I have my eye on the stout stick I hope to grab to crush the big

101

snake. When I finally get it, I warn the head that I mean to fling it at the beast, although I don't believe I can stun it with such a puny club. The head watches my struggles with a little smile, he himself has the mask of a large snake – that he hasn't yet killed me or had me killed perhaps means that he has given up his monstrous project. But I – I want him dead.

16 July 1999
Le jour où je n'étais pas là

This time you came my love, came among the heaps of chaotic dreams and perilous adventures. We met at the hairdresser's, her home-salon. That day everything a mess for our hostess: the employee makes a brief appearance in the dream, and goes off without finishing the job. Left in the lurch, the customer starts to moan. For the owner, a charming woman who has other children and the whole house on her hands, this is a big problem. I keep an eye on the child, who slips under tables and sinks, plays, shows drawings, leads a life parallel to that of the cat, which, for its part, comes and goes, squeezing under the neighbours' fence – towards the vegetable garden, each time batting at a shape on the left, which doesn't budge and I wonder whether it is a real animal or lump of clay until the hit thing raises its snout: it is indeed an animal, a sort of mini koala. The owner offers to take me. She will give me a new hairdo, she says. With four clips she pins my hair back on both sides. That's all. It is you to whom she shows off her handiwork my love. Do you approve? I'm not convinced, this hair so black and also a little frizzy underneath, flat on the sides. You polite. Do you like it, sir? asks the owner, implying she thinks you my squire. And I, I savour the naturalness with which, not bristling, you play the role of someone entitled to an opinion. Off we go. Here we are the two of us face to face and very very close in an office, papers spread around us, we talk at length on the telephone, without any telephone, in the closeness of the telephone. I ask you 1,000 questions you respond at length, in detail, about what I've written, about death, life, us, I make notes, notes, short of paper short of time for this tidal wave of wealth, I scribble notes on every single page of my notebook which fills up in all directions, wherever there is room at top speed it's as if I'd suddenly gained access, the open door to your heart and genius and it's boundless, everything I wished to know, commentaries, corrections, and I am even going so far as to speak to you since it seems we have time, we are not to be cut off – of the hurt I have suffered for years, the jealousy, I mention it to you, as if to a doctor healer, confident, and now you listen and say nothing. Which I interpret as: 'You know perfectly well that's your business, you make that all up, I don't have to answer for what exists solely in your head.' Or so I tell myself. Then we must leave this place, it's time.

August 1999

In our lives everything is separation passion and union right to our drawers we are one.

Peep of day and the end of the year, we were still snug in bed when the house filled with noise, everyone had come. Eve was there too to mark the day. Gently we untangled our limbs. We were not yet dressed. We stood before the cluttered table where Eve sat with her papers. She was saying that Madame X had retired, it was official. As she spoke I saw your notes spread on the table. Dismayed she could see his words and papers everywhere, I slipped something over them. He went out for a moment, Gentleness itself, to dress. Returned to whisper that he had filched some titbits. It was delightful and tender, and I told him I would get him some breakfast right away. I was dressing, I had put on a T-shirt and said I didn't have any underpants. So my darling himself went over to my drawer and drew out a pair of black pants. It was a gesture of incredible delicacy, a lover's attentiveness. The year drawing to a close, we were about to part. So my love also took out his blue and white bathing trunks, which were attached to my pants – and holding them up (I was sitting on the bed pulling on my black pants) he said: don't forget these next summer. Yes, my love, I'll take them, your trunks tied to mine, if I can't have you, to the shore. We exchanged signs of intimacy then and there and in parting the most secret joined us.

29 December 1994

'The End.' The finished book comes to the end without end. The book I've written on us, just before the big party we are throwing in secret, everyone against us. The two of us are in the bedroom, on the bed, and I show you the book that talks about us. You are with me until the last chapter which recounts 'the end', the wedding. The one I am preparing in secret. You have reservations. You disagree with the interpretation. Several times you allude to it. I search for what's wrong. Did I embellish things? Lie? I'll rewrite it, I tell myself, I both don't want to fuss over it, don't want to be indocile either. The helper turns up a little late, come to give a hand with the party – says she is just out of hospital – quickly I go into the kitchen with you. The house has a corridor the old one Avenue René Coty. I tell her what to do. Eve is there too. What bothers me is Omi also is coming. It makes too many. But Eve says stop fussing, Omi is already in the kitchen cleaning and no one cleans so fastidiously. She will do it to a tee. All the same I run to the sea it's my ritual.

There she is, outside, big thick green rollers a mixture of Mediterranean and ocean. I know you have to plunge in. I walk to the edge, the waves don't want me. Finally I dive. Here's my mother as well, like in Algiers. Around her lots of fish, good-sized, a hand or two, swimming along the edge. She bumps into one. Ah! They say that's good luck. I come back to the house. I come back without stopping thinking about the end of the book business. I wake up and realise what I've forgotten: it's the pigeon. I am the second pigeon, with the plucked neck. That's what was missing. I'd finished the book a few days ago or rather the book had petered out like a wave on the sand. Done. Ever since it has gone on sending signals. I sleep, it wakes me up, it dictates to me, rectifies, recalls. It's already three nights past 'The End'.

11 August 1999

Delightful Annie tells me – we are out in the street of this 'Italian' town – that she has just met a very cultivated young man who lives on a barge on the river, who has read everything, she praises and praises him and says he's someone you should marry. He's thirty-eight. She tells me his name. It's a name I recognise. I turn to Anne. He's a person who's written me several times. I'm thinking thirty-eight that's more for Anne. But Annie doesn't notice. On we go together we enter the Palace, which has an amphitheatre like the Sorbonne, huge, or like a courthouse, still empty, a lecturer is expected. In the hallways I run into some 'fans', a distinguished older woman, who adores me, and her daughter or someone like that. An extraordinary drama unfolds in the Palace. A crime. The local Prince who looks so nice and who is talking at great length with Anne (or flirting) is really a murderer. He's had someone assassinated and this person who'd disappeared is here: in the strange latch of one of the gallery's deep windows. Compressed, the body is shut up in a cylinder and every time somebody opens the window they in fact twist the box the cadaver is shut up in. I am aghast. A handsome rosy-cheeked young man comes along. It's my letter-writer. He tells us he's the one who discovered all this during his military service. Now the Prince is threatening him. Anne staggers out of her interview. She comes towards me, pale, says she has to talk to an analyst immediately, I think she could speak to me, but it's better like that but who? I tell her to talk to the elderly fan who has eyes for me alone a nuisance but I don't see who else there is on the spot. After we'll see – Anne exits with the very nice older woman. The Prince steps up to the podium. Now he's been found out, he's going to explode, and the world is on tenter-hooks.

Thursday 12 August 1999

You at last! Him, me, us, in our glory.

There we were on the beach of the world it is a great boulevard and we were walking side by side, taking long strides, naked, equals, like two morsels of god, incredibly brilliant and just as well known. I was stunned to see us run such a risk. We could have walked separately but side by side and as we walked it happened our bodies freely touched. Whereupon you say, with a laugh but also wary, that you knew the room earlier was packed with the arch rival's spies (who? was the Spy someone or the public?), you'd felt it and me too in the tremor that ran through the crowd people who think it but don't say it, besides when you entered the room, someone actually came out and cracked a joke and Tranet pointed at your belly, said its paunch was proof enough. But Tranet is a tool of the arch rival. So you think they suspect. Well now, here's proof, even you make no bones about it and we go like gods, I mean brimming with silent laughter, our triumph. It filled me with a world of joy. Walking like two columns of desire.

13 August 1999

In the crowd around the display of goods on the table, I saw the man, a wretched workman, but perverse, pinch a tangerine from Anne's little pile of purchases. But I tell him this has been bought, can't you see it's wrapped up. Not the least embarrassed he helped himself to two more. A thief I saw. In a fit of helpless rage I snatched one of the tangerines from his hand scratching him. But nothing stopped his thieving. Anne had only two or three pieces of fruit left. Later the man showed his not inconsiderable talents. He robbed the museum, and if he was caught, played terrible tricks. Thus a friend of mine found himself glued to the wall when a precious manuscript grew sticky all over. Impossible to free my friend. Save by ripping up the precious white book. Which is what I did. I began tearing off pages. Then I realised the evil fellow must be hiding in the wall. I rapped, in vain. One of my companions took a small pointed object and stabbed it into the surfaces of corners. Yet the man couldn't be far, gripping and manipulating the sticky book. Our companion whipped around and jabbed at the far corner. There, a cry! Ah! he must have struck the devil in the eye! Lucky it wasn't me I thought, exulting at the blow. We'd show this evil-doer.

1994

I had agreed to give a seminar abroad so Fatima and I were heading for the building where they were expecting me. Outside, a crowd. My audience? I approached, thinking all the while what to say. I had a few ideas. In any case I had to get to know them. Who will I be talking to, the all-important question. I would ask them, I thought, to fill out a card, and that would enlighten me. What's the culture? What's the difference? And the sexual difference? A few questions to help me get to know them. I greeted a group, some of them seated on the ground. I told them I was on my way back from Asia (I did a Cambodian bow and spoke about dress in various regions), that the men wore loincloths and not the women, that the introduction of pants for women was recent, which made you wonder how underwear began – (but I had no answers) and that in the old days the men were naked under their loincloths. That was it. Then everyone got up and walked towards a building, was this for me? I tagged along. The building I found was made entirely of metal bars with wrought iron above which gave it a pretty oriental look, but it was a sort of scaffolding, and rickety, which did not reassure me. If it collapses I thought as I picked my way along beams and catwalks, we will die, especially if we are high up, although below we could be crushed. I asked Fatima. Is this it? Yes – I was not pleased. The people found their places in the stands. I went on down anxiously, I would have preferred to change. What kept me going was the thought of giving an excellent seminar. Picking my way down I saw them carrying in a sort of podium and stage with bright red couches, it was for me they were attaching it like some sort of swinging throne, you'll have something to eat too someone called. Them all smiles. There I am going down. Now the awful surprise – I'd expected this sort of metal amphitheatre to be full. But once below I saw that only the left quarter of the room was full. A shock. For the University that had invited me too it was disappointing not to fill the space. Well, I tell myself, it's the first session, afterwards word will get out and with a bit of luck everybody will come for the second. All the same, as I realised how things stood, I felt prepared for the worst.

15 June 1998

One noon

This was towards lunchtime when everybody was waiting around in the hallways in the rooms of the restaurant – I myself was in front of the kitchen counters, about to snitch a bit of cucumber from the jar in which it marinated.

That's when the lion appeared. No doubt it came by mistake or because it was young. When I saw it I went over. It was a pretty golden beast, heavy, not very big, with a firm, resolute and fearless gait, I bent and stroked its head and body. It was a baby still sure of itself and without experience of evil and content to be in my hands. But not everyone felt so, many were afraid, a stupid ugly girl came over and shook a bunch of whips under my nose to scare the beast away. Brusquely I pushed her off. And made haste to pet my lion to reassure it and make up for her nastiness. Then I asked for milk. Alone with it I poured it some milk as best I could into a sort of bowl and I introduced it to milk. I dipped its muzzle to the bowl and it began to drink. It was good to be able to be good to a little lion.

3 December 1996

The imitation of love

Everybody was busy upstairs in the house, each at her task. M. was going up and down, I myself left the child whom I preferred to forget about up there in the care of old J., what can you do with an ugly late-born child that doesn't talk. You give it something to eat. I never gave it a thought. People came and went. I saw R. again who spoke to me with that combination of niceness and arrivingness of the arriviste. I went so far as to confide in her (were we seated on a bench?) did you know I had a little girl a year or two ago? She expressed a lively interest. We climbed to the top of the house. My nasty little girl greeted me with mute signs of joy, she was mongoloid. R. found her extremely vivacious. She lay on the chest. She delighted in every-thing, refused nothing, she was full of curiosity and good will, I ended up saying, she is not pretty, she looks stupid, but underneath there's a great deal of intelligence. And truly she understood and expressed everything in her way. Love above all. Everything I didn't give her she rendered in love. In the end she observed everything I did or thought and mimicked it, this was her way of thinking, to imitate, using her body. So when I lay down on the bed, the poor naïve thing began to mime a lover's gestures, she twined her arms around my neck, she kisses me everywhere, and she even ends up taking my left breast in her graceless little lips and sucking, the way she'd seen it done. This bothered me a little, but I admired her daring. Considerable power lay hidden under her apparent muteness.

Messie

In this huge fair, big as city sprung up for a day, everything keeps us apart and everything unites us. The miracle, or our luck, is that despite everything we manage to meet and toss off fiery words. So it is that late in the evening, after days crazed with people, I can join you in your room, despite the presence of Al. and her friends. As things stand there's no way she'll call me in my room. So late in the evening, I head off through the immense empty luxurious rooms of this endless hotel, and racing through deserted reception areas, on wings, I cross the spaces to your room. What keeps us apart is just days obligations the world obstacles. That's how amid the great crowds of the fair, carried away by love's fever I find myself next to you in a packed metro train that I shouldn't have got on, but I was unable to let you go. The line covers vast distances very fast. We are pressed together and surrounded in the little car, there is old Marguerite, J.-P. Audigier is with me. Really I should have stayed in and prepared for that evening's inauguration. But I was going back. At the stop, suddenly, your voice close to me, as if it were my own, calling soundlessly, in my very being, I adore you I adore you I adore you. In the noise of machines and people the words are softly shouted, a little anxious, it is God's gift and as the automatic doors eject me I shout me too because what else can I say. Then fired up and hurrying, I retrace my steps to my room where I must prepare to meet you again in public later. But who knows the speed of a magic metro. What took the machine ten seconds becomes interminable distances. With J.-P. A. we race along corridors, platforms, like a station that never ends and thronged with people, he suggests the staircase – I say that that would be worse, cramped and the crowd to slow us down. We run like crazy we run, time passes – will I get back in time to change, here we are scaling cliffs of furniture, skirting the abyss, the void next to a heap of wardrobes, I crawl dizzy and clinging to narrow ledges, barely avoid falling, in a while we find ourselves in courtyards, in sculleries, walls everywhere save for a slender opening we slip through the rubbish disposal, this is the back of the hotel. Now all we have to do is cross these inter-minable reception rooms where I am accosted by unknown women who want to give me theses to read, discussions, more time wasted, I have trouble making headway, will I ever get there? At last here's the floor, the room. But events have changed the scene. The room is bare, no ceiling, it sits in a hollow. Up above all around passers-by and voyeurs. I am seen, and from above. How to change my clothes? Well, too bad. I undress as if I were in my room. I strip off my pants. I keep a black T-shirt on – fairly long – I shall dress quickly and elegantly. I've been spared nothing. But still that night I managed to join you. And your ardent words are in my life, I adore you I adore you Iad I you

25 March 1997

When one doesn't know (what) one is dreaming

In the cold house of Monday, the weather is awful it seems, I get ready slowly, unsettled, it is bright, Fatima cries out strangely suddenly I remember, I ask her where is your baby, how is it, she has just given birth, she doesn't answer, she retreats into shy silence, I realise things are not going well, but where is it, in the hospital, perhaps it won't live, oh how sad, oh, if only one could make another one on the spot, I try to get ready, I tell Eve to get out her lancet, in the big room. Thessie goes wild, what she has in her mouth, grooming it vigorously, is a yellow Indian cushion, she holds onto it by the corner with a tiger she nibbles at, moans, chews doesn't let go. Eve wants to save my cushion, but I intervene, don't you see she wants her little cat, she has her littiger in her mouth and she can't let go, oh dear oh dear, for sure she has lost her little cat – and now she's been spayed – so she clings to the littiger painted on the pillow, she'll never ever let it go.

9 January 1995

Strange waking with snow

Someone woke me, I believe it was that good little priest, I emerged from my bed I get up, it was freezing – my bed is beside a wall of glass, suddenly I see a shower of white petals, what am I saying – snow! A delightful sight the window was full of it, but I look up and I see the top windows are open, I start to close them, there were more and more of them, when I had closed everything standing up in my nightgown the glass door opened and without the least embarrassment in come two people and their child, neighbours. I am stunned I think there must be a mistake, but not at all, these people begin to look around my house without a sign of embarrassment. I am furious. I shut the door. Then I tell these people where to go out. In the absence of any haste on their part I utter some words of reprobation. At which point the woman starts to claim they have a perfect right to enter like this, etc. No, really. I put an end to the discussion and show them the door. Still in my nightgown I head for the shower. It is in the corridor, small as a wardrobe. In comes my brother very cheerful and full of bluster. I was about to take a shower. He cuts me off and tells me he wants to introduce me to someone. One minute I say I'm having my shower. No, says he right now, she doesn't have time she has to leave. What do you mean doesn't have time, it takes me two seconds I say and to show I mean what I say I undress. Vexed my brother tells the young woman never mind we'll go and celebrate your graduation elsewhere. I dart a glance at her before attempting to slip into the closet. She's very young. I say all the same you could wait a minute. No, she's got two seconds and she's off again. My fault, I suppose? I have to obey and not wash just because he turns up with his latest and wants to introduce her? No – I squirt shampoo into my hair, I have a helmet of froth through which I make out the girl's features. Pure youth red lips over a big fleshy smile. My brother's got a lolita. But she has to go home, fast. Can she come to your seminar? See, if she'd stayed she could have met Ashley (Ashley enters the dream) and Eric who are on their way over and who could have looked after her. But it's not in the cards. I try to rinse myself. You have to stick your

126

head in under its cap of foam, there's not much water,
it takes a while. Everyone's out of sorts. It is snowing
this morning.

12 January 1998

Hedgehog adoption

Finally I arrived at my friend Elizabeth's. She had changed her life. She was living in a large bright apartment. And she had animals. In particular she had adopted some hedgehogs. I wanted to see them. It was mealtime as it turned out. I was dying to see them. I took the plate that had been prepared. And I slid it under the table to lure the animal without scaring it. It kept me waiting an instant. Softly we called it. At last I saw it coming. Slowly, a big hedgehog made its appearance. I didn't want it to run away. It inched up. Later Elizabeth sets out a big meal, a great sheaf of leaves, there was also cabbage, vegetables, she makes quite a fuss. This hedgehog was a likeable boy, he stretched out on me and I liked his free and easy ways. I wanted to adopt him. There was the other one as well. I spoke to him and he replied nicely. True there was Thessie. This hedgehog was like her in some ways, you see. I wondered if this wouldn't complicate matters or not too much. The hedgehog, since I'd shown my interest in him was much bigger, clearly an affectionate little boy hedgehog.

11 September 1995

This was in a big hotel where he and I were invited to a meeting. The joy of being together and feeling as one was constantly threatened. From without from within. At dawn I woke a little late, already 7:30 when I left my room and I saw the students, all ready, heading to the dining halls. Whereas I was barely up. I hurry. I'm not dressed yet. I came ill-prepared for this meeting just one not so elegant outfit and what's more I'm drowning in it, I'm having a terrible time dressing, as I go along the paths, hitching up my baggy trousers with one hand, while in the other I have my mobile phone. I flounder on. Now you call me oh beloved poet. I'm on my way I tell you. Getting myself together grows urgent. You speak from your room, with the intensity and depth I love. To add to my floundering I want to note what you say in my book as I walk, I flick through it. You launch into a reflection about yourself the way I love. You speak to me of sociality and let me tell you say you the socialists are tyrants. Meanwhile on the path clutching my too-big trousers I leaf through my notebook and find something jotted 6 June that I'd forgotten. That was a few months ago. I said: is it therefore necessary to accept a relationship with a whole mixture of people, a note which reflected my distress and anxiety, when I'd thought that what was inescapable was precisely to accept the beloved's complexity. But that's all over and done with. Right now you say such wonderful things that I can't bear not to write them down. So I lie to you, for love I tell you, 'We keep getting cut off – it's the mobile phone. Let's hang up. In a moment I'll be in the room and I'll call you.' 'Me too,' you say naïvely, 'I'm having the same problems with the mobile.' So in a second my love. It's because I don't want to miss a crumb of my beloved's thoughts. I rush along. Now I am in front of the hotel. I go in at last. I am a little lost. Ill-dressed, I walk past one of the nice receptionists who says hello. I thought I'd find the elevator but it's not here. Never mind I walk into the lobby: there I'll figure out where I am. In the great velvety reception rooms I recognise nothing. Where oh where is the main elevator? I daren't ask. This is ridiculous. I've been here a few days. My self-esteem won't stand for this. Time passes, it's been at least twenty or thirty minutes since I broke off that precious conversation with my love! He must be wondering where I am. Am I not to find my room? Serves me right for having wanted to cut him off, for wanting more, more, a little robbery, now I'm the one who's robbed.

9 April 1997

Children, absentmindedly

I was at home with all the children, Pif Anne includ-
ing Thessie and the youngest half-cat half-little-boy.
And you came as planned. I was a little under the
weather so I was ever so slightly languishing on the
bed. But we weren't really undressed, like the last time.
You were tall young strong good my love. We weren't
all that free because of the to-ing and fro-ing of the
children who could come in and who went to the
bathroom or asked me things. Nevertheless it was
voluptuous. I was on my side but my black skirt
undone. You exclaim: look at your hip, it's gold. The sun
falling on my hip had gilded it. How lovely you are you
say. And what about you! Still we restrained our desire
because we had agreed that would be next time, but we
revelled in it already, in advance. And you, you were
there already, oh how good it would be, we rejoiced,

and we spoke of the children. The last one was on my mind. How strange, I was saying, I hadn't really noticed my pregnancy, yet there he was my youngest, a lusty, headstrong babe. Sometimes one makes babies like that, on the side, absentmindedly, especially when they're lateborn. Maybe we'd have another? The house was a hive, abuzz with children, the light entered with its promises of delight, we lay on our sides towards the delicious future.

22 November 1995

Thessie my concern

Initially, it's because she starts playing with the electric wires that run around the top and bottom of the room, she cuts them she chews on them, she yanks at some creepers, but afterwards it's because she discovers the mysterious attraction of plugs: I see her put her paw out and stop her in extremis, but I have constantly to keep an eye on her. I scold her several times so she's aware of the danger. But promptly she does it again I think only of her, I cuddle her, I look for her, sitting in the stands when people squeeze in next to me, I ask them to make space for my cat.

Then, it's when I try to come home. I take my wisp of a car, I drive down the avenue and instead of taking the first on the right, I take the second, that is, maybe the last for it has an incredible name, 'street of the bears monkeys and others', maybe because I'm a person who looks as if she knows where she's going. But when I turn into this street it's a trail in the forest with coarse bare blonde sand punched with sinkholes, and who knows if I'll ever reach the end. I'm driving almost at ground level. From which to my astonishment loom up, as the name foretold, incredible creatures, sorts of bears small monkeys that lie down ahead of us for a joke, little sand creatures crabs or spiders big as my hand, and then the bear, the bear I see in the distance and wonder what's going to happen to Thessie whom I've been hugging meanwhile, the great big real mummy or daddy bear, coming closer and closer. I inch along now we are right beside it, no collision, what an outing. Cross my fingers I make it!

22 October 1997

The alarm has rung. I shut it off. I dream the alarm has rung. I am in my bed and I don't want to get up. Turning my head, I see a big spider dangling over the pillows – in the centre of its web, not far from my face, and a few other insects that weave my nights and my awakenings. Ah, something for Thessie I say. Day already. My aunt and my mother go shopping, I stay on the bed. I call Thessie, asleep across from me, on my chair. Thessie! Thessie! Here are some beasties for you. She comes. Sees the huge spider. Leaps on it. They do battle. Thessie is all business.

Such is my response to the attacks that fray my sleep each night: the ongoing horrible thoughts about the little fellow, the threats, webs woven over our beds. On my left the pillar of life. Across from me Thessie who at 7:15 still hasn't budged. She watches me write my strange waking. Because the night was so bad I couldn't get out of it by the first door. Once the alarm cracked day open I had to go back to the dreams for help. That's how I came to call on Thessie.

Who is she, she whom I call on to clean things up? Me?

24 October 1997

General de Gaulle paid us a visit. We were all were in our rather improvised camp in the forest. He spent the day in the common room, talking with us. When he stepped out for a minute, I went over to the window that gives on the forest and we exchanged impressions. I had noticed I hadn't seen his nose. He had however behaved like a nice old man. When he came back we went to the local shop together. How poor such places are. They sell a bit of this and a bit of that. If I lived there I might be forced to make a grab for the two books in the middle of sweets and flies. The old man wanted to give me some token gifts, I picked out a few small items and half a box of wild strawberries. Because I was afraid to take too much. But at the end when it was time to gather it all together and pay, I nevertheless took the rest of the wild strawberries. Out we went. De Gaulle and I and the others made our way along the woodland paths. Then we reached town where he got his car to take me back home or somewhere. His car was special, a sort of big convertible armchair you slide yourself into after raising a Plexiglas roof. Not bad. I sat down beside him, I had my things, my bag, I was elegant. He drove off in reverse. Still, after a few minutes I was surprised: were we going to drive down the whole of the main street in reverse? The other cars faced forward, and we hadn't turned? But De Gaulle replied in town here it's permitted, no cause for complaint, of course, some people might find it difficult to drive backwards at the normal speed, but for him no problem, it was just fine. And on we went, in the tide of cars going down, we went down, but the horses' heads faced back uphill.

20 May 1998

Frankreich

Omi, Pauline, Eri had just turned up, what a hulla-baloo. I heard their voices. Just then Eve entered my room and started to complain what a nuisance they already were. After a moment I cut her off and, as if the danger and the event had suddenly come back to me, I ordered her out with a sharp look and a phrase. Mummy, mummy, Jesus is here, go, go. Taking fright she darted off. But too late: on her way out she found herself face to face with baby jesus. So what I was hoping to avoid came to pass. It wasn't the end of the world. In fact jesus showed tremendous aplomb. He acted natural. He greeted her like a friend of the family, as if all was as it should be. He was divine and simple, in a white shirt, no jacket, light trousers. He followed me into the bedroom. You could see the three of them across the way gabbing like magpies. I vaguely explained to jesus that they weren't expected, that Eve had forgotten to warn me, she had forgotten everything. My beloved had just returned from a trip. And he had set his things down in my room, his letters. At that moment the door to the bedroom opposite opened and Pif appeared. He hadn't seen jesus for such a long time. Astonished and happy to see him, he hesitated a moment. An adolescent face with its youthful squiggle of mustache. He looked uncertain and resigned I tell him come, come and say hello. He advances smiling. Funny to see the two of them standing there with their mustaches greeting one another. Come on, I said, enough boytalk, we've got work to do. Pif withdrew. Finally I was alone with my darling. Jesus lay on the bed sighing. On the chest of drawers I saw some letters – a yellowish envelope belly gutted, on which he had written my address, and I gazed at the word *Frankreich* in his familiar handwriting. He was back from Germany. I wondered if he had written me, if he hadn't sent it, perhaps he had taken the card from its envelope to give me now? I longed for it. Lying on the bed you murmur. 'You know my love everything is false.' Reverberating the sentence wakes me. Who was it addressed to? Then it says (the sentence): 'Dream I tell you.'

15 September 1997

142

Translator's Note

How to translate a dream? How to translate words jotted down in the dark as the dream darts off like a fish caught and released; then, years later, hauled up to the light of publication, untouched up by the dreamer? How to keep the roughness, the quick-glimpsedness of the thing? An almost impossible task. The translator's temptation is to polish – how much more difficult not to do this when the text is a first-and-only-draft, a dreambook what's more, whose language is doubly foreign. I have tried to keep these 'limbo things' alive on the page, to preserve their omissions and repetitions, slippages in time and space, in pronoun, in focus – their disconcerting strangeness – in the hopes that they would retain in English something of the shimmer they have in French.

Beverley Bie Brahic